Courtesy Ira Rosenberg - Detroit

This is Skeezer, who helps to heal emotionally disturbed children. She lives and works at the Children's Psychiatric Hospital at the University of Michigan Medical Center at Ann Arbor. Skeezer's job is to reach troubled children who have retreated within themselves and become resistant to human help. Carefully trained, but responsive in her own way, Skeezer makes her comforting presence felt by a child starved for affection, by one who wants just to be listened to, and by those in need of a playmate.

Now in her seventh year of residency at CPH, Skeezer is the trusted and beloved member of a medical team, carrying out her mission as "canine co-therapist." Her story, portrayed with poignancy by one of America's most skilled storytellers, is one of dedication and delight in duty.

SKEEZER
DOG WITH A MISSION

CHILDREN'S
PSYCHIATRIC
HOSPITAL

BY ELIZABETH YATES

illustrated by Joan Drescher

Harvey House, Inc., Irvington-on-Hudson, New York

Copyright © 1973 by Elizabeth Yates
Illustrations Copyright © 1973 by Harvey House, Inc.

All rights reserved, including
the right to reproduce this book
or portions thereof in any form.

Library of Congress Catalog Card Number 72-92687
Manufactured in the United States of America
ISBN 0-8178-4992-0

Harvey House, Inc., *Publishers*
Irvington, New York 10533

Foreword

THE decision to institute residential care for the disturbed child is never an easy one. Mental health workers would always prefer to treat the youngster and his family as outpatients or, if necessary, in day treatment so that the family unit is kept essentially intact. It remains, however, that some children do need psychiatric hospitalization and, for the most part, they are quite seriously disturbed.

At Children's Psychiatric Hospital we are fortunate in being part of a large University Medical Center. We have many students from many disciplines. Stagnation is impossible because new ideas and innovations are constantly being fed into the system.

Skeezer is perhaps one of the better examples. There had been many pets at CPH, but generally they were of the categories of fish, rabbits, guinea pigs, hampsters and even occasional baby birds who needed care. When the idea of having a dog live with the youngsters was proposed, my immediate response was negative. I love dogs and have owned many since my childhood, but my initial worry was twofold. Certainly it would be essential that no child, however disturbed, would be hurt by a dog. Second, it was essential that whatever dog might be chosen would have a "good life" at CPH. To attain both goals seemed impossible. Not to attain them would be unacceptable.

When it became clear that our staff wanted to try and Dr. Cohen, the veterinarian, said he had the dog, I had little choice. Miss Williams, the Head Nurse on Sixth Level where Skeezer took up residence, deserves special credit. As is obvious in the book, she is a dedicated woman and would be first to give credit to others for the health and care of not only the children, but of Skeezer. It remains, however, that she sets the pace for Sixth Level and has been instrumental in insuring Skeezer's success. Very few Head Nurses are asked whether their resident canine can have a litter of pups on her ward. She agreed and proceeded to help Skeezer through her pregnancy and delivery. She also became "Head Nurse" to a rollicking group of puppies. I'm sure such techniques are not taught in Schools of Nursing, but I'm equally certain that many young people coming into the field would know them as Miss Williams does.

Some might feel this book is partially fiction, but it is only as far as names of the children are concerned. Many dedicated mental health workers are not mentioned by name, but I'm sure they will enjoy reading about Skeezer. At a recent meeting of the staff there was a discussion of a youngster's pre-admission visit to the hospital. The nurse mentioned that the boy had been nervous as he toured the ward, but that "Skeezer gave him the full treatment as she lay on her back inviting to be scratched on the stomach."

I'm very pleased that my staff had the intuitiveness and foresight to see the value of having Skeezer and also grateful to Elizabeth Yates for having done such a good job of describing her. I can only hope some young people who read this book will be motivated into the mental health professions.

STUART M. FINCH, M.D.
Director, Children's Psychiatric Hospital
University of Michigan Medical Center
Ann Arbor, Michigan

vi

Contents

1

What It's All About

THIS is the story of a dog who is a working member of a hospital staff. Referred to as a canine therapist, Skeezer may be the first of her kind in the country; and, as the first Seeing Eye dog opened up a new way of life for the blind, Skeezer may be doing the same for disturbed children. CPH, short for Children's Psychiatric Hospital, is part of the University of Michigan's Medical Center. The children who come to this hospital need help in handling their emotions.

Fear, anger, guilt, frustration, inadequacy — any of a dozen causes — have resulted in serious behavior problems; and the reasons are many.

Some parents, meaning well, have just not understood what parenthood is; others have been baffled by their children's personalities; and some just haven't cared. Often emotional problems have been compounded by physical problems and children are in as much need of medical help as of psychiatric. Whatever it is that has made things go wrong for the children, their inner turbulence has made it impossible for them to cope with life.

They have come from all parts of Michigan, from busy cities and farming communities, from all types of homes. They have been referred by family doctors, school authorities, and sometimes juvenile courts. Treatment begins the moment they arrive; treatment that makes them feel they are loved.

Alice Williams, the nurse in charge on the Sixth Level, says to her staff, "Without love we'd only be patching up, trying to put them together with adhesive tape. Love is their need. With some of them, the lack of it in their early years has been as hurtful as the lack of good food. There are children who have never had a story read to them, never been sung to sleep by a lullaby, never been talked to as having minds of their own. When they come to us, these are the ones for whom recovery is often the longest.

"Take a cue from Skeezer. Watch how she feels her way into a relationship and does what she can do. You may learn more from observing a child's reaction to her than you will from studying that child's reaction to a Rorschach test. Often, especially when they first arrive, they can't seem to share their troubles easily. Skeezer acts as a means of communication. That's a great deal of what she's all about at CPH."

Some children are taken by surprise when they see a dog in a hospital, but the surprise is rewarding. Skeezer becomes a link to a world they have left behind or to a world they have never known. Either way, comfort or adventure is promised by her presence. They soon learn that Skeezer can be confided in and won't talk back, that she likes to be cuddled up to, and that she doesn't mind being pushed around. She doesn't know anything about their problems. What she does know is that each child that comes to CPH is her charge.

Since her first year of residency, Skeezer's home has been on the Sixth Level with Miss Williams and her staff and the children there. CPH has two other in-patient wards which Skeezer visits in her own time. Because some children at war with themselves and their world have periods of violence, CPH was built to be indestructible. Doors to unsupervised areas open only for Staff with keys; windows have special screens. Those on the south look toward other buildings of the Medical Center, those on the north across fields to the Huron River. There is an easy air within the green-tiled walls: no uniforms are worn, voices are soft, movements unhurried. The days are slow-paced. Time is carefully planned, but there are no pressures.

Nourishing meals at regular hours, rest, play, study, all combine in the treatment that enables children to come to terms with themselves and build the self-respect that has been damaged or destroyed. The atmosphere is one of friendliness, of helpfulness. People say *Yes,* but they can as gently say *No* and mean it. Children feel secure, knowing where the line is drawn.

They go to school every weekday morning in special classrooms on the Second Level. An hour at first — at the most two — is all that some can take. The time increases as gains are made. Eventually some of the children go to an elementary school in the neighborhood and are away the better part of the day. There are hours for OT and RT (occupational therapy and recreational therapy).

Each presents its challenge: to muscular control as hands make things, to behavior as group situations are entered into.

Three hours every week are spent with a psychotherapist. This time of talk, of play, of sharing has special significance. The therapist may seem to be like a parent, or again like a big brother, often more like a good friend. With him, or her, the child who is deeply troubled and withdrawn, or the one who explodes quickly into anger, feels at ease. He knows that he can be himself and that his therapist will understand.

It may mean many visits, many hours, as a way is found to the mind that has shut itself off from all approach and as mixed-up emotions begin to be straightened out. When the therapist asks the child not to bite or kick because it hurts, not to scream because it makes ears ache, the child gradually realizes that there are valid reasons behind simple requests. The therapist is a person with feelings, too, and the child's attitude of "I don't care" and "I'll do what I want" becomes less attractive to him. It is a long way from self-will to self-worth, but on the way, consideration for others begins to make sense and responsibility becomes something to strive for.

This is the pattern of life at CPH. Within it there is ample time for the children to be themselves, to follow their own pursuits, to play with each other. They know that their sickness is in their minds and they are honest about it, eyeing each other with fellow feeling rather than criticism. Aware of one of their number who has gone into a tantrum and has had to be restrained, they may say quietly to one another, "He's really sick." When they go home on weekend pass they may be teased by their friends for living in a Buggy House. They won't deny it. CPH is to them a place where they are understood, where they feel safe and secure. While there, they will not be asked to do anything beyond their ability, and someone will always be near to help. They know they are gaining, even though the ways are small. They know, too, that a time will come when they will be able to return to their homes, stand up to stress and cope with life.

The children in this story, called by names other than their own — Rosey Ann and Walter, Bentley, Oriole, Willie-John, Gwen and the others — are all actual children who have been at CPH at different times.

"But they look like children anywhere!" a visitor exclaimed to Miss Williams.

"Of course." It was not the first time Miss Williams had heard that remark.

"They look so tidy, so nicely dressed, and they're so thoughtful. That tall dark boy with the white turtle-neck shirt held the door for me."

"Aaron? He came from one of the most deprived areas in Detroit." Miss Williams smiled. "The children are sharp at testing visitors, as you'll soon find out, good at wearing their emotional tuxedos. That's a phrase the psychoanalyst, Dr. Fritz Redl, uses. Even so, social behavior and good grooming are all part of their therapy. It's one of the ways that respect for themselves is instilled, and some of them have never had much."

"Aaron's conversation was lively. I expect he's one of the gifted ones."

Miss Williams shook her head. "Liveliness is often used to disguise lack. Aaron has a potentially high I.Q., but he was so deprived of any mental stimulus during his formative years that the damage has left gaps too great to be repaired. He's been here longer than most, but he will not be able to learn to read, or to learn academic subjects, unless new methods are discovered. What others acquire by reason, Aaron will have to do by guess."

The visitor watched Aaron walk down the hall.

Skeezer came out of one of the rooms and joined him. The boy placed his hand on her back. The dog lifted her head toward him as if listening to what he was telling her.

2

Rosey Ann Arrives

THE ward was quiet, or almost so; the children had gone to bed, lights had been dimmed. Clicking on the terrazzo floor was the sound of Skeezer's nails as she made her rounds: into one room and up to a bed, snuffling at the figure hunched down under blankets, drawing her tongue across a hand hanging over the edge of the bed, not staying long in any room but going on to the next. At one door she paused. Muffled sounds were coming from under the pillow that had been pulled over a small head. "I want to go home — Mummie, Daddy, come get me."

Skeezer's nose worked as she sifted the smell still new from the many that were familiar. Slowly she crossed the room to the bed. Resting her head near the pillow, she nuzzled under it inquisitively. Wet cheeks were not unusual to her, nor was the taste of salt. She licked until there was a response, a turning of the head, a breath indrawn quickly. Skeezer lifted a large front paw and laid it on the bed, then she took an edge of the pillow between her teeth and tugged at it. A tousled head emerged, a hand crept up to cover the paw.

"Oh, Mickey, I'm so glad you're here."

It never mattered to Skeezer by what name she was called. All she cared about was the sound of a voice.

Rosey Ann moved over to make room. With ease of custom, Skeezer was up on the bed and stretching herself out alongside its occupant. There was a choked sigh, then another kind of sigh with a rumble in it as the two snuggled close together.

A nurse, one of the two on night duty, making her rounds, saw that Rosey Ann was fast asleep. One arm was flung across Skeezer, also asleep. "You know what they need, don't you, Skeezer," she said as she reached down to stroke the dog.

There was no sound in the darkness, no move-

ment that could be seen, but a stub of tail quivered
and then was still.

Rosey Ann Anderson had visited the hospital
several times with her parents. They had talked
with doctors and nurses, the psychotherapist who
would work with Rosey Ann, the social worker who
would work with the Andersons. Rosey Ann was
eight but small for her years, and picture-pretty
with a fay quality about her. Easily frustrated, the
fay soon became the fiend and she lost control of
herself. She had been in and out of hospitals and
guidance clinics for most of her years, as her particular problem had been difficult to diagnose.

On the day she came to CPH to be admitted
as a patient, she was uneasy and frightened. She
clung to her parents and dragged her feet stub-
bornly, looking as if she might at any moment fly
into a tantrum. Then she caught sight of Skeezer
and her mood changed, "There's that dog again!"
she exclaimed, hopping up and down with excitement. Letting go her hold on her parents' hands,
she skipped away to play with Skeezer.

Miss Williams led the Andersons to the room
that would be their daughter's and while Mrs.
Anderson unpacked the small suitcase, Mr. Ander-

son related their recent difficulties with Rosey Ann.

"We try to explain things to her but she won't listen. Yesterday she ran into the street and was nearly killed. If we punish her, it makes her more stubborn. If we reason with her, she becomes hysterical; but we want to learn how to help her."

Miss Williams listened attentively. "You will," she said quietly, "and Rosey Ann can be helped."

When the little girl came running back to join them, followed by Skeezer, she demanded attention. "You know what? Skeezer put her paw on me and asked me to scratch her stomach. Then she laid down and waved all her toes at me so I'd keep on scratching her."

The time soon came to say good-bye. The Andersons eased the parting with their promise to come every weekend to see her.

"Are you going to leave now?"

They nodded.

Rosey Ann reached out one hand to feel for Skeezer. Sure of her presence in the room, she lifted her face to be kissed.

Caught up in a flow of events new to her and surrounded by other children, Rosey Ann scarcely realized that her parents had gone. It was soon time for supper at which she sat quietly, pushing the food around on her plate and eating little; then it had been play time and she had entered into the games, experimentally at first, soon with abandon. The taking of showers followed, the getting ready for bed, the snack of cookies and milk, her own room and the dimming of lights. It was only then that Rosey Ann fully realized that something had happened.

Where had her parents gone? Why weren't they here to tuck her in bed? Why was she in this strange place? Was she to be here forever? In the closet her clothes were hung as they had been at home, her other things were laid in the drawers of the bureau. Her pink and yellow bunny was on a small chair near her bed, her music box and some picture books were on the window ledge. It must be that her parents were never coming back. She scrunched herself tight together and pulled the sheet over her head, then burrowed her head under the pillow. With eyes squeezed shut, lips puckering, hands pressed over her ears, she began to cry.

It was then that Skeezer had reached the door of her room, made her own investigation and decided that this was the room where she would stay. And it was a few moments later that the night duty nurse had discovered them both.

At some time during the night, Skeezer left Rosey Ann and retired to her favorite place half way down the long hall. There her doghouse stood, though she rarely sought its shelter, and her bowl of water. She liked to lie up against the cool tiles with her head toward the door. From this vantage point she could survey both ends of the ward and move quickly into action if need be. In the daytime, a visitor coming in the entrance door would send her racing to it to bark in inquiry or greeting; a sound at night meant a raised head, pricked ears, and then a return to sleep if her presence was not required.

Before going off duty, one of the night staff took Skeezer outside for a brisk walk. By the time they returned, the kitchen lady had arrived and started preparations for breakfast. Skeezer stood in the doorway and drew attention to herself with an imperative bark, then she went off to visit some of the rooms. By the time she got back to the kitchen door there would be food in her dish.

Most of the children were already awake. Some had started dressing. The new one was still asleep. Skeezer nuzzled her gently, then drew her tongue across the hand that rested on the sheet.

Rosey Ann's eyes opened. She stared, blinked,

then smiled in recognition. "You're not my Mickey, you're Skeezer."

Skeezer went on down the hall, but in a few moments she had returned. She stood in Rosey Ann's doorway.

"You've just come back to see if I remembered to stay awake. Well, I did!" Rosey Ann pushed the covers back and got out of bed.

The day at CPH had begun.

"Tell me about the little girl who came in yesterday," a new staff member asked Miss Williams.

"Rosey Ann is perceptually handicapped," Miss Williams began in her quiet-voiced, straightforward way. "Her inability to distinguish between letters like b and d, p and g, is only one of her difficulties. Up and down, left and right, round and square are others. She sees, but what she sees can not be made meaningful. To coordinate hands and feet is, just now, beyond her. The result is frustration — "

"Followed by anger and hysterics?" the staff member asked.

"Exactly. Her parents are kind people, intelligent, and they love her dearly; but they could not understand for a long time that Rosey Ann had a real problem. So they were not giving her the concrete attention she needs and the slower pace of living."

"I suppose they thought she was just being willfull."

Miss Williams nodded. "Even now, I'm not sure how clearly they grasp what the situation is. When they left, they told Rosey Ann they would be back every weekend. The child probably could comprehend the words, but she could not conceptualize the amount of time that will pass before she sees them again."

"Did she panic?"

"No, and we may have Skeezer to thank for that."

"Leave it to Skeezer!"

Miss Williams smiled. "You can't imagine how often I think that, especially during a child's first days at CPH. In non-stressful situations Rosey Ann will do all right, but she's apt to get confused when too many stimuli come upon her at one time."

The staff member looked thoughtful. "So, we don't overload the circuits."

"Right. While Rosey Ann is here, we'll slow her world down to a pace she can handle, a pace that may vary from minute to minute and from situation to situation. We'll let her be with a group as long as she can take it, but we'll make sure that there is always someone near to move in when a one-to-one situation is called for."

"You can do that while she's here, but what about when she goes home?"

"In all cases, the social worker plays a crucial role. She has already seen the Andersons and will see them every week. They will be in therapy as much as their child; all parents are. While Rosey Ann is learning to cope with stimuli, her parents will be taught to recognize the areas in which she gets confused and acts impulsively. When she can go home for weekends, her parents will have learned how to manipulate her environment to her advantage."

"This won't happen soon."

"Oh, no. Rosey Ann will be with us for some time. She has much, very much, to learn. So have her parents."

"What can we hope for?"

"Everything! Past experience encourages us to think that children like Rosey Ann can overcome their handicap. And there's much in her favor. She has a bright mind, her health is good, and her parents want to help her. Parents are our greatest asset, make no mistake about that."

"But it will take time."

"Yes." Miss Williams spoke as if that was in good supply at CPH. "Time is our ally."

3

Worth a Try

SKEEZER had made a link with Rosey Ann from her own home to CPH; each place had a dog.

When Thomas arrived and saw Skeezer stretched out on the vinyl-covered couch in the day room, his first words were, "At home, our dog isn't allowed to get on furniture." But from that moment, Thomas knew he was in a place where rules were not unreasonable.

The day Tillie came, Skeezer had cut her paw in the playground. When Tillie saw Miss Williams washing and bandaging it, she had the feeling that the same would be done for her if she should ever be injured.

Ron had had no experience with animals and when he saw the big black dog he was frightened. But he did not stay frightened long, for Skeezer's cool nose soon fitted itself into his hand, her eyes looked up at him, and her stub tail began to wag. Ron was surprised. She acted as if she liked him and he had not done anything to win her affection.

The children accepted Skeezer. The grownups asked questions about her. Her being part of the hospital medical team was a story that went back over seven years.

As CPH serves a threefold purpose of treatment, training, and research, its doctors are constantly exploring new approaches to healing. In their meetings they had often discussed the use of animals; and small ones like gerbils, hamsters, fish and birds had been used in limited ways. Children found them fascinating to watch but there was no way of relating to them. Then someone suggested a dog.

"Impossible," was one reaction.

Murmurs were made about behavior and sanitation.

"Worth a try," was another reaction.

There was general agreement that children who could not get on with people often could with pets and that the try might prove to be beneficial.

The Animal Research Laboratory of the University was asked to supply a dog. After a short time, Dr. Bennett J. Cohen sent word to CPH that he thought he had the right one. She was a female of uncertain breed, five months old, and untrained. Dr. Cohen explained that he had observed her for several days. He had watched her in action and noted how well coordinated her movements were; he had watched her when she was watching him and he felt that her strong stance and steady gaze indicated sound nerves.

"Dignity coupled with ruggedness is there," he said, "and even though she's still a pup, she's deep-chested and strong-boned. Look at that skull! It's large enough to hold a good-sized brain, and she's got a powerful jaw."

"What makes you think she's the one for us to try at CPH?"

"She likes people," Dr. Cohen answered, "and she responds to the attention given her. She shows every evidence of having spent her first weeks of life in a good home. A dog is like a child. They develop societal ways early."

The dog cocked her head, moving her ears forward, then back.

"She's had plenty of affection as well as cod liver oil," the vet said, running his hand over her back.

"Where did she come from?"

"Who knows? She was found by the police a month or so ago, collarless and half-starved. They made every effort to locate an owner but no one came to claim her. They took good care of her and when they brought her here her coat was as glossy as it is now, her eyes bright, and her ribs were beginning to get covered. See how alert she is? She wants to get going."

"She's worth a try," was the cautious answer.

The dog lifted her head as if waiting for a command. She looked from one to the other — the doctor who knew about children, the veterinarian who knew about animals.

She had the Doberman's markings and the breed's air of nobility; her fearless gaze seemed to suggest a stalwart spirit. She had the Labrador's button ears and sleek muscular body, but not the tail, for hers was bobbed. She had the German Shepherd's dense coat and the expression in her eyes hinted at the breed's ability to use good judgment.

"There's an accumulation of great brains

there," the veterinarian said as he fondled her well-shaped head, "for the strains that have gone into her are noted for their intelligence."

"I don't imagine that her immediate ancestors have done anything in particular."

"Perhaps not, but memory is long. Give the dog something to care for and instinct creates the motivation. Give this one something to do and watch her do it. She'll merge her will into her master's. She'll accept the charge of children as her ancestors did the charge of flocks of sheep or herds of cattle."

The doctor reached down to stroke the dog.

The dog's eyes moved from one man to the other. Her tail was poised. She was interested, but uncertain.

"Don't expect too much too soon," Dr. Cohen said. "She has to do some growing up of her own first."

Taking hold of the lead and whistling softly, the doctor from CPH left the veterinarian's office. Once outside, the dog pulled him to a stop as she insisted on sniffing at grass and bushes. At the curb, they waited to cross the busy street, then walked between the many-colored poles on either side of the entrance way and into the CPH building.

At the elevator, three nurses were waiting to go up to the ward and the dog greeted them as if they were all old friends. When the elevator door opened, the nurses stepped in but the dog held back.

"Come on, Skeezer," one of the nurses said.

The dog stepped forward, followed by the doctor. The door closed and they all rode up to the Sixth Level. Within a matter of minutes, a stray mongrel had a name, a home with a family, and a job.

From the first, Skeezer wanted to romp and bite and chew. Noisy and demonstrative, she ran up and down the hall with the children, into and out of their rooms, tumbled in play with them, then collapsed in sleep. Her bark was boisterous. She recognized no difference between grass and trees, floors and chairs; but she was quick to learn, once she got the idea and provided someone was near who recognized the moment of her necessity. Her high spirits could have proved her undoing. It was clear that she would have to be trained to passivity if she was to fulfill her function as Resident Canine at CPH.

Miss Williams took Skeezer home with her for five days to begin her training.

During the next weeks and months Skeezer made mistakes. She was guilty of misbehavior and earned her rebukes; but as her training progressed both at home and in the hospital, she began to grow into her work as she grew into her body. The paws no longer seemed big and clumsy. The bark was deep but it had meaning: she wanted to go out, she wanted attention, she was greeting, she was warning. Gradually she discovered that it was more important to do what she was expected to do and so win approval than to have her own fun-filled way. She knew what Miss Williams' low-pitched whistle meant and, bobtail wagging with pleasure, answered it. She began to understand specific commands. By the time she was a year old, she had a fairly clear idea of what her work was and how she was to go about it.

Watching her as she stood solidly on all four feet, poised and ready; watching her as she ran with her charges, body movements in perfect balance, Miss Williams saw her as an evidence of what the children came to CPH to attain: radiant mental health and its buoyant physical expression.

The doctor who had said "Worth a try" was willing to admit that the experiment was working. "But only time will tell," he added, "whether a dog

can really help disturbed children."

About that Skeezer had nothing to say.

She knew that she was receiving the attention she craved; that she needed children as much as they needed her. She was not aware of any unusual performance on her part. She was simply doing what she had been constituted by her breeding and recent training to do, and that was to protect and to companion.

4

Skeezer Has Her Puppies

SKEEZER had a particular friend, a Siberian Husky, Chukchis, who belonged to a medical student living off campus. Chukchis was brought over often to romp with Skeezer in the playground to the delight of the children. One day Miss Williams said, "Skeezer and Chukchis are going to have a family of their own in a little while."

Some of the children wondered how this would happen; others thought they knew.

"Will there be many puppies?" Thomas asked.

"Yes, there could be."

"What will we do with them?"

"We're going to find homes for everyone, even

before they are born." Then Miss Williams went on to explain to the children about a female's six-month season. When Skeezer arrived at hers, she would be ready to accept Chukchis as her mate. "Skeezer is eighteen months old now. That's a good age for her to have her family."

Skeezer enjoyed Chukchis's frequent visits. Their games were lively and rarely included any of the children. Then Skeezer began to grow coquettish with Chukchis and, soon after, she offered herself to him. The dogs frolicked as they had before, but this time their capering had significance. Skeezer accepted Chukchis's attention, demanded more, and soon the two were tied in a canine embrace. The children who happened to be watching from the windows of the Sixth Level and witnessed the event were intensely interested.

Calendars were marked for the prescribed sixty-three days and Skeezer received more attention than ever. Chukchis made no more visits and Skeezer gave no evidence of missing him. For the first few weeks there was no indication of the future; then the big body showed signs of growing bigger. The teats began to swell and take definite form. Skeezer was not so ready to play with the children, and the time came when she preferred no

play at all. Her expression changed. A dreaminess came into her brown eyes. Lying in her familiar place in the hall with her back against the wall, she moved her tail slowly when the children knelt beside her to feel over her body for the life that was forming within it.

Skeezer had her own house, but she used it infrequently and now not at all. It had been made when she first came by the ward's office clerk to whom the children often looked for help. Its outside walls had been painted to make them look like brick with windows added, shingles had been painted on its roof, a pretend chimney and TV aerial were attached. Old blankets made up its furnishings. Among them were a few battered toys, an elephant without a trunk, a horse with three legs, a stuffed frog that had lost most of its stuffing. Some of them she had taken a fancy to during her puppyhood and snitched from the children; some she had been given.

Now that she would soon have a family of her own, the house had become a symbol. It was given an address. *866 Puppy Lane* was printed over the door in clear black letters. The numerals were the University's departmental code for requisition slips from the Sixth Level, Puppy Lane was the children's choice.

Now, in O.T., the children were building a whelping pen from specifications found in a dog book. Boys and girls sawed boards and hammered nails in readiness for the event. Each one felt a part of the whole process; each one relished telling Skeezer what was being done for her.

Miss Williams' office, which had a window in one wall that opened on to the adjoining office, was thought to be the best place for the birth, so the pen was placed there. Its floor was covered with newspaper that had been shredded by the children. The preparation took time, but everything was ready when the sixty-third day was checked off on the calendars.

Early that morning Skeezer had begun to show signs of uneasiness. Led to the pen and persuaded to lie down in it, she soon started licking herself vigorously. A group of children took their seats at the window in the adjoining office and watched, spellbound into silence. The first puppy came at six-thirty and Skeezer was deft in her care of it. Gripping with her teeth the sac that enclosed the puppy, she tore it open, then licked hard to dry the puppy and stimulate its breathing. Hardly was this done before another arrived. And then another. When the shredded papers began to get messy, one of the staff exchanged them with careful hands.

Time passed. The children changed places with other children so all might have a chance to share in watching their dog give birth. It was comforting to them to see that Skeezer knew exactly what to do, tucking the tiny bodies up to her teats and encouraging them to suck. The puppies knew, too, and kneaded her body energetically with their front paws, then drew the flow of milk into their bodies.

By nine o'clock nine puppies were feeding. Any one of them could have been cupped in a child's hand. Their eyes were sealed, their ears were like little flaps close to their domed heads, but their mouths were in action. Skeezer had an abundance of milk and only eight teats, but no one went hungry. Places were shifted. Full puppies, with milk dribbling from their lips, rolled over in a huddle of sleep, while hungry puppies groped for and found the source of supply.

The children watched and wondered, whispering to each other now and then.

"And they've all got homes waiting for them,"

Tillie said in a hushed voice, "nine puppies, nine homes."

"Did I drink milk from my mother just the way they're drinking from Skeezer?" Rosey Ann asked.

"Just like that," Tillie said.

"Not just like that," Aaron suggested.

But Rosey Ann was quite satisfied. "That's why I love my mummie."

When the puppies were all accounted for, Skeezer was taken out by one of the staff. She stayed only long enough to take care of her needs, then back she headed to the elevator and up to the Sixth Level. A plate of food was offered her and she ate hurriedly, then returned to the pen, flattened herself out and let the nine wander all over her. Nuzzling them to her teats, she cleaned them by licking while they fed. Every now and then she glanced up proudly at the watching children.

Birth announcements that had been prepared beforehand could now be completed and sent out —

Chukchis of Snowland

and

Skeezer of Mergatroid

announce the arrival of nontuplets

on Sunday, July 23rd, 1967, between

6:30 A.M. *and 9* A.M.

6 male, 3 female

Visitors Welcome

The children soon had the puppies named: Momsickle, Popsickle, Smokey the Bear, Swinger, Linus, Trinket, Mischief, Pixie, Sprite. Some took after their father and were unmistakable Huskies; some were tiny replicas of their mother.

In a week they were squirming and wriggling around the pen; in two weeks, with their eyes opened, their ears flapping, their teeth appearing through pink gums, they began to try to clamber over the sides of the pen. Within another week, the first one made it. Waddling out of the office and down the hall, it was followed by another. Soon all nine were yipping and puddling and pouncing on whatever offered itself for play, nipping fingers and shoes and toys. The O.T. carpenters had to get busy again, this time building barriers to keep the puppies out of the bedrooms.

At five weeks, Skeezer's milk supply began to dry up. As it did, the puppies' appetites increased. Soon they were eating solid food and nibbling biscuits, but showing little distinction between food and whatever was around to sink their teeth into. They raced up and down the hall, played with each other, with their mother, with the children, then tumbled into heaps of sleep.

From the mating, through the birth, and into puppyhood, every phase had been explained to the children. Most of them had had distorted ideas of the process involved in procreation. At best, birth was a mystery; at worst, there was something nasty about it, associated with bad words, closed doors, unsatisfying retorts to questions, whisperings in the dark that became smirkings in the light. Now they had seen how one form of life got its start, came into the world and took hold. They would not soon forget how Skeezer had looked when she freed one small puppy, then another, from its protective sac, licked it dry and into being.

Their questions were answered for the time; their curiosity was appeased. An elementary understanding of sex replaced their misconceptions. It was not dirty. It was natural, as natural in its way as the rising of the sun.

"Nobody wanted me the way Skeezer wanted her babies," Tillie said to no one in particular, though there were half a dozen children in the day room at the time.

Often they paid no attention to each other's words spoken at random.

Jessie, crayon in hand, was filling in spaces in a coloring book. When she had finished her page she crossed the room to the couch. "Scootch over, Tillie, and let me sit beside you."

Tillie moved to make room.

Jessie put her arm around Tillie. "I guess we wanted you at CPH."

As the puppies grew and Skeezer's actions with them varied from attentive mother to rowdy playmate to swift disciplinarian, the children were aware that she played no favorites. All received her care, her attention, her rebuke if deserved. She could be plenty rough and increasingly she had to be as the puppies grew in size and strength, but her discipline was never wanton. It was the obstreperous pup who got a bat from her powerful paw, the stubborn pup who was pushed along by a thrust of her nose. And no one ever received more love than another; each received all she had to give.

By the time the litter had attained the age of two months, most of them had gone to the homes that were waiting; two or three stayed on longer as their owners worked at CPH and could come in every day to play with them. Skeezer seemed ready to part with her puppies. This was a marvel to the children who had suffered from overprotectiveness. Skeezer was not going to hang on to her children. She had brought them into the world, cared for them during their first weeks of helplessness, played with them, disciplined them, taught them what they needed to know to get on with their lives, and now she was willing to let them go from her.

When the last one was finally carried away, Skeezer stood in the middle of the hall and watched; as the door closed, she turned around to face the children who were also watching. Going up to them, she deliberately bumped into one after another to see who might be interested in a game.

"Come on, Skeezer, I've got a balloon for you to pop," Aaron shouted as he raced through the hall and to his room.

The others followed, their shrill voices interspersed with Skeezer's gay barking.

A few weeks later she was taken to the veterinarian for the simple operation that made certain there would be no more puppies. Skeezer was a dog with a mission, and the mission was care of the children in her charge.

CPH would never be quite the same again. The children would change as the years went on, but there to stay and often to be referred to was the memory of the time "when Skeezer had her puppies."

5

Skeezer's Real Family

By the time she was two years old Skeezer had settled into her work. The training she had been given brought out the best in her three strains; the surroundings satisfied her; and her recent experience was to her advantage. Having brought up one family of her own, she had proved that she knew what young things required — play and quiet, discipline and love, in equal measure. The family at CPH was now the one she accepted as hers.

The Sixth Level would always be home base; but Skeezer's visits to the other two in-patient wards were made frequently and according to a time-table of her own. When inclined to go calling, she went to the door at the end of the hall and reared up on her hind legs; then she thrust her forepaws with her seventy pounds of weight against it. She expected it to open and generally it did. There were times when it was locked and she had to make her intentions known by a series of short barks, different in tone from the bark she made when an urgent need of her own necessitated out.

"Going visiting, are you?" one of the staff asked. The key, worn on a lanyard, was fitted into the lock and turned. The door swung open and Skeezer marched out on her self-appointed way.

On her own now, she went toward the elevator and sat before it until it arrived and the door opened. She had learned that this was bound to happen as there were always people coming or going throughout the building. She got in and rode to the floor she wished to visit. Her attitude to the children in another ward was the same as to those on the Sixth Level: interest in all, favorites with none. She gave more of herself to new arrivals for a few days, unless they were children uncertain about a dog. When this was the case, she waited to let them make their own approaches, although she had ways of encouraging them.

Often, when staff member or visitor stood

waiting on the Sixth Level for the elevator to arrive, Skeezer would be the only passenger to emerge when the door opened. A flick of her ears, a wag of her tail and the person's presence was acknowledged, then she walked to the ward door and sat before it until it was opened. Her return was announced with a series of barks, for Skeezer was always glad to be back where she belonged and where the one to whom she owed full fealty was in charge.

She took her visits away from the Sixth Level seriously; the children took theirs in the spirit of fun.

The times they rode with Skeezer in the elevator were times when they were on their way to the level that led out to the playground, or to the park along the river. The playground was a safe and happy place. It was surrounded by a tall wire mesh fence that kept balls from rolling away. It had swings and slides, a sandbox and picnic tables, a water bubbler. On their way down to the playground, the children's spirits were high with expectancy; on their way back they were still apt to be high with excitement. Skeezer was generally the quiet one. Sitting on her haunches or, when there was room in the crowded elevator, sinking all the way down and putting her front paws out so she could rest her head on them, she waited.

To the children, the journey was a game, especially exciting if the door closed and the elevator started to move before anyone had pressed button Six.

"Where are we going?" Rosey Ann asked.

No one had an answer. Obviously someone had pushed a call button at another level.

The elevator came to a stop and the door opened slowly. Instinctively the children looked down at Skeezer. Alert but relaxed, she made no move to get up and go toward the open door. The visitor, waiting in the corridor of the Fourth Level, saw there was no room. With a smile and a wave of the hand, she indicated that she would wait for the elevator's return.

"It isn't our level," Tillie announced.

When the door closed, no hand moved up to the panel but all eyes were on Skeezer.

"Where are we going now?" Aaron asked as the elevator started to move.

"I pushed Five," the staff member in charge said.

The elevator came to a stop. The door opened.

Some of the children held their breath. Skeezer yawned.

The door closed again. Staff pushed button Six.

When the elevator came to a stop and the door opened, Skeezer rose to her feet and walked out first.

"Skeezer knew! Skeezer knew!" the children shouted as they rushed to greet Miss Williams who was standing at the open door to the ward.

Hands fluttered over Skeezer's back, rested on her head. "Good dog, Skeezer. Good dog."

Eager to tell Miss Williams of the fun they had had, they clustered about her, chattering gayly.

"When me and Skeezer were playing tag, she was IT and she kept trying to get me!" Ron's voice was shrill with excitement.

"When we were walking in the park by the river," Thomas said, "Skeezer kept going in the water and I splashed her, then when she came out she splashed me all over!"

Supper time was near so the children were soon racing down the hall and into their rooms to change shirts or dresses, comb hair, and make themselves ready for the next event of the day, but one of their number lingered.

Putting her small hand against Miss Williams's skirt and looking up with a face filled with wondering, Rosey Ann asked, "How did Skeezer know when we got to the Sixth Level? 'Cause she did."

Miss Williams shook her head. The same wondering that filled the little girl's face was in hers. "I don't know, Rosey Ann. We'll just have to tell each other that's Skeezer's secret and leave it there."

Rosey Ann nodded. She was satisfied. Skipping down the hall, she went to her room to tell her pink and yellow bunny about Skeezer.

When the children went into the dining room, Skeezer did not go with them. This was a place where she had no authority. There was a barrier across the doorway visible only to her, and past it she never went. It had been one of her first lessons and it had been strictly enforced. She took the children's meal times as her opportunity for undisturbed sleep and retreated to her place midway down the hall. What went on in the dining room was no concern of hers.

Anticipated as meals were, and relished generally, the dining room was a place where emotions easily got out of control, especially at noon time when the children returned from school.

"I read three pages today and Aaron couldn't even read half a page without help," Nathan announced. "He's really stupid."

"I'm not," Aaron said, making a face.

"Stop making a face at me or I'll punch you in the mouth."

"I didn't make a face at you. You're a liar."

"You did too!"

"Didn't."

"Did."

The harassment might have gone on indefinitely had Thomas not started shuffling the bread around on its plate to find the best piece. Seeing

him, Nathan reached for the bowl of French fried potatoes and emptied them onto his plate. Three pairs of hands immediately shot out toward the potatoes, grabbing at them not to eat but to throw at each other.

"Simmer down, kids," staff intervened. "Better go to your room, Nathan, and change your shirt. Wash your hands, too."

Nathan stamped out of the room, muttering that he was never going to eat there again.

Ron was the first to settle into the business of eating. Thomas did after he had poured gravy into his milk and puddled it around with a spoon. Aaron picked up his fork reluctantly. In his past, fingers had served often more than silverware and when events triggered an upset, the past had a way of taking him over.

They ate in silence.

"What we need is some rules," Ron said.

"Rules," the two others agreed.

When Nathan returned, hands washed and in a clean shirt, the others told him they were going to make up some rules for the dining room.

"O.K. When do we start?"

The four who had bedeviled each other put their heads together and began their project. Later that day, with colored crayons and a large sheet of paper, they printed the rules in letters big enough to command attention and be read by all who could read. Miss Williams gave them permission to tape the paper on a wall in the dining room. The boys then went off to O.T. feeling that all was in readiness for supper.

DINING ROOM RULES
1. No put-downs.
2. Good manners.
   - a. mouth closed
   - b. no finger pushing
   - c. silverware manners
3. No kicking chairs.
4. Feet off other chairs.
5. No swearing.
6. No copying or mimicking.

The first time any of these happen, you will be excused to your room until someone comes to talk with you.

Tillie, when she saw them, said, "I'm kind of glad Skeezer can't read."

The rules worked fairly well. Since the boys had made them for themselves, they realized that they would have to impose them on themselves. The dining room became a quieter place, though it still had its moments of upheaval.

The girls got together and decided to draw up a set of rules for the day room. They worked over them for a week, then with help from a staff member, lettered them on a large piece of cardboard and hung it where it would be sure to be seen.

YOU MAY NOT DO BAD THINGS
1. No fighting, swearing, kicking, scratching, slapping, socking, spitting, etc.
2. No tickling or silly behavior.
3. You may not scream or yell.
4. You may not stand on tables or each other's toes.
5. You may not take off your shoes or put your feet in other's faces.
6. You may not blow on your arm to make noises.
7. You may not take or destroy other's property.
8. You may not stick out your tongue.
9. You may not kick the table.
10. You must go to the bathroom before coming to play games.
11. You may not pull or hang on Staff's lanyards, or pull off their glasses.
12. You must eat with good manners, not bubble milk or pop, and if you burp you must say "excuse me."
13. You may not interrupt someone speaking.
14. If you break more than three rules you must go to your room.
15. No tattling.

Skeezer had her rules, too. The one that kept her from the dining room was among the many that had been learned during her first year at CPH. But there were occasions that demanded new ones. When she began to get plump, even though the children insisted that she liked being that way, tidbits and snacks were ruled out. Skeezer had work to do, work which required her being in good condition, and she was well paid for it. Affection was the currency she valued; her bonus came in balloons.

6

Walter and the Two Messages

WALTER looked sullen and acted tough the day he arrived at CPH. The only change in his expression was when he caught sight of Skeezer. He had been drawn to her on his first visit and was relieved to see that she was still there. His parents, who thought they had given him everything, had never given him a dog.

After supper, when Walter went to his room, he saw that someone had gone there before him.

"Skeezer, you're on my bed!"

Skeezer looked at him, her stub tail moved.

Walter closed the door. A relationship was in the making; perhaps the first meaningful one for

Walter in all his twelve years.

The children accepted Walter as one of their number, but when they called him by his name he turned on them angrily.

"Don't call me Walter, don't don't!" His voice got high and his cheeks flushed.

He avoided them for the first few days; they took the hint and left him to himself. He was determined to live in his own world, but Skeezer was equally determined that he should not live in it alone and followed him everywhere; except into the dining room. Then she went to his bedroom.

Walter Miller, Senior, was a contractor. When Walter, Junior, became a part of the Miller family, the sign over the office was changed to read *Walter Miller and Son, Contractors*. Walter, Junior, came to know that the word "son" was meaningless.

The Millers had no children, but since everyone around them had children, they had decided they should adopt one. The agency to which they turned suggested other outlets for their interest in young people — Boy Scouts, Future Farmers. "Everyone else has children, why shouldn't we, even if we are getting on in years? We can give him everything." Finally they succeeded in their intention.

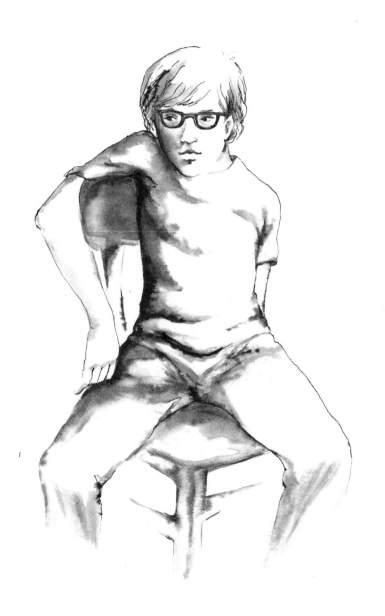

And they did give Walter everything. The best care, the best food, the best clothes. His room was the only one in the house to be air-conditioned, for his parents felt it important that he sleep as well in hot weather as in cold. A cough, a sneeze, an ache, and off he was taken to the doctor for treatment; then he was kept in bed, waited on, worried over until he was well again. When he developed asthma and had to fight for breath, the Millers were alarmed; but medication provided relief.

"You should be very grateful to us, Walter dear, for the care you have received."

At ten he was given a bicycle for his birthday. "Ride it on the sidewalk, Walter, and don't get your new pants dirty."

"Yes, Walter dear, you can go to Sam's party, but don't overeat."

"Of course, you can stop at the library on your way home from school, but get only books for your age level."

Walter wondered why his mother couldn't say just *one* thing, why she always had to say two.

It was the same with his father.

When Walter referred to one of his friends as a "damn nice kid," Mr. Miller was furious. "Walter, I know that I swear, but I don't want you to until you're eighteen."

"Like smoking?"

"Well, not exactly, but you can smoke when you're eighteen."

Walter held himself tight. He knew that tears were not to be indulged in and that anger was frowned on as unbecoming to a well-brought up boy.

There were no simple directives in his life. Everything said was doubled, "Do this, but don't do that." There was nothing that was not in some way conditioned. And there was no love for its own sake. Always he was reminded that he should be grateful for what he had been given. As the adoption agency had foreseen, the Millers had little understanding of what it meant to be parents and Walter soon got even with them for their ignorance. Chafing at the restrictions that surrounded him, he found ways to revolt.

A series of fires bearing every evidence of arson were at last traced to the Miller boy. To the horror of his parents, Walter coolly admitted his guilt.

"But Walter, we've given you a home and a name to be proud of!"

Walter shrugged.

Shoplifting followed. When Walter was faced with his guilt, he admitted it.

"But, you can have anything you ask us for, Walter."

Then it came, and not in the privacy of the Miller home but in the publicity of Juvenile Court, a temper tantrum followed by a flood of tears. The torrents that had been repressed for years were loosed. The Millers were obliged to face the fact that their adopted son was a delinquent. An understanding judge referred the boy for psychiatric treatment.

When Walter was led from the courtroom by a marshal, he did not protest, nor did he look back at his parents.

"Can he be helped?" they asked the judge when they sat with him later in his office. "We always tried to do the best we could for Walter."

The judge looked at them kindly. "Let us hope," he said.

When the Millers left, the judge voiced the thought that had been in the minds of many of their neighbors, "They would have been better off with a pet."

Walter was not sure what name he wanted to be called by at CPH as long as it was not the name he had been given.

"They want me to be like him," he said bitterly to Miss Williams. "They think they can make me into a person like him." He would never say the word "father."

"Walter," Miss Williams explained calmly, "it's not what you've been, it's not even what you may be, it's what you are now that matters to us here."

"Not 'dear' then," he said in a low voice, spitting out the word as if its taste were bad.

"Just Walter," came the assurance.

Skeezer put her head on his knee and gazed up at him.

"You're just plain dog," he said to her. "Nobody tries to make you into anything else. Nobody tells you to do this and not do that."

Walter's attachment to Skeezer made him want to know all about her and he often questioned the children. "Tell me about the time when Skeezer had her puppies."

They told him in their different ways, recalling what had impressed them most.

"When she knew a puppy was hungry and needed milk, she would draw it close to her," Rosey Ann said.

"She could push a puppy away, too," Aaron added. "And, man, when they began to get big, was she rough! She made them mind and they liked her for it."

"Was she really their real mother?"

A chorus of voices shrilled to her defense, "Of course!"

When Skeezer got up and walked away, Walter pursued her down the hall. "Wait, Skeezer, I've got something to tell you." He threw his arms around her and dragged her to the floor. She submitted to his attention, listened to the words whispered into an ear; but when she had enough she got up, shook herself, and walked away. Walter did not follow. She was headed toward her refuge in the nurses' office. There, behind a desk, she was safe, for none of the children entered that room without permission. As Skeezer had her invisible barrier at the entrance to the dining room, they had theirs here.

The county 4-H Club announced that it was sponsoring an Obedience Class for dogs to be given

by an instructor from the Ann Arbor Dog Training
Club. Skeezer was entered in it. She could never
be entered in an American Kennel Club dog show
as she was not a purebred, but this was something
different. Few, if any, of the dogs would be from
recognizable breeds but all of them meant a great
deal to their owners and would mean even more
when they were trained. The class was to be held
on eight successive Thursday afternoons at the
nearby Saline Farm Council Grounds. Walter was
chosen as the one to handle Skeezer.

He was surprised and very pleased. No one
said, "You can handle Skeezer but don't let her run
away."

"This afternoon," Miss Williams announced,
"we'll take Skeezer to the vet's to have her teeth
cleaned and her nails clipped."

Half a dozen children piled into the station
wagon for the visit to the vet, but that was only the
beginning. Every day for a week before the class
commenced they took turns in brushing her. They
knew how important grooming was to them and it
carried over to their dog.

Aaron surveyed her after one of the last brush-
ings. "You look mighty smart, Mrs. Skeezer. I bet
it makes you feel good inside to look so shiny outside."

71

Walter had been looking forward to the class but on the day itself he was nervous. Standing in the field with nine other dogs and their handlers he glanced back at the sidelines where the children from CPH were sitting. One or two hands waved. Walter nodded and swallowed hard.

Skeezer, intensely interested in all that was going on, was calm. Assurance, commonly communicated down the lead to the dog, went up the lead to the boy. To the staff watching with the children, the trainer's opening remarks seemed similar to the teaching they had been given. "Be quiet in voice and manner . . . It is the tone that will carry, not the words . . . Be generous with praise when deserved, firm with discipline when merited . . . Let your dog know what to expect . . . Give a single clear command, then wait for it to be acted upon."

The first lesson was the basic one and the dogs seemed to learn as much from being with each other as from the trainer. "Call your dog to heel. Name first, then one short sharp word. Jerk on the lead if necessary to get attention. Expect to be obeyed."

"Skeezer, HEEL!"

The children on the sidelines watched the

marvelous spectacle of Skeezer walking round and round the ring, her nose close to Walter's left knee, doing just what she should and doing it better than any dog there, from the smallest who bore resemblance to a Dachshund to the largest who had the conformation of a Saint Bernard if not the coat.

A single command was mastered at each lesson, then practiced during the week on the Sixth Level. Never had Skeezer received so much attention or so much praise for what she had been doing reasonably well most of her working life. "Skeezer, COME!" "Skeezer, DOWN!" "Skeezer, SIT!" "Skeezer, STAY!"

Like a theme song at every lesson came the trainer's words, "Say your dog's name once, then give the command once. You don't want to confuse your dog in any way. Let the dog know who the master is or he'll take advantage. When the exercise is over, tell your dog he's good, fondle him, play with him, then bring him back to attention."

The last of the eight Thursdays would decide what dogs had done the best. Excitement bubbled over at CPH. Walter woke up with a stomach ache and said he couldn't go to the Council Grounds that afternoon. The children howled with disappointment, but in their way of rapid change soon forgot.

Walter, also, forgot his stomach ache; but in the afternoon at the Council Grounds he held up a finger wearing a Band-Aid. Skeezer's lead was placed in his hand. Eager to get to the ring, she jerked and Walter had no time to protest. Whether he wanted to or not, he had to go where Skeezer took him.

While the class was forming, Walter turned suddenly and left the ring with Skeezer. "Look," he said to a staff, "my Band-Aid has come off. My hand is too sore to hold the lead."

"Oh, we'll soon fix that." A box of Band-Aids was produced from a pocket and the finger was soon rebandaged.

The names of dogs and their handlers were being called. Walter and Skeezer turned back to the ring as a chorus of good luck wishes followed them from the children. Standing in line, they waited as one dog after another went through an individual performance. Walter, watching, knew that his dog would do better than any dog there, but he dreaded taking her into the ring alone. He slid his hand down the lead to rest on her head. She looked up at him. Her stub tail wagged.

"Walter Miller and his dog Skeezer Merga-troid."

Taking a short hold on the lead, Walter moved into the ring. One after the other Skeezer executed the commands he gave her, heel, come, sit, stay, down, heel. She was as self-assured as he was nervous. At the conclusion of an exercise she would look up at him quickly, and once she drew her tongue across his hand. As on the first day, she conveyed her own calm. The fear that had made Walter feel as if he was tied up in one big knot began to loosen inside him.

The last exercise, the Figure Eight, was the hardest, but to a dog and a boy who had performed up to it without fault it presented no problem.

The judge called to two helpers to stand facing each other about eight feet apart, then indicated that handler and dog were to weave around them to make a figure eight. "Take Skeezer off her lead and put her in position. When you are both ready, give the command and proceed."

"Skeezer, HEEL!" Walter's voice was firm. Together they advanced toward one standing person, worked around him and advanced toward the other. "Heel," Walter said again, even though Skeezer was doing what she had been told to do and needed no reminder; then, as if to encourage her, added the command "Come." Completing the exercise, he brought her to a halt before the judge.

"Praise your dog."

Walter did lavishly. From the sidelines the CPH children clapped and shouted their praise of Skeezer.

When all the dogs had done the final exercise, the judges compared their score sheets. The names of the three highest were called and asked to come to the center of the ring. Walter and Skeezer were placed between a small brown dog resembling a poodle whose eyes never left her mistress's face and the languid Saint Bernard. To the poodle went the blue ribbon, to Skeezer the red, and to the biggest dog the yellow.

Walter was pleased but puzzled. "What did Skeezer do wrong?"

The judge put his hand on Skeezer's head as if to make amends for his decision. "Not a thing. She did what was required. It was you who gave her a double command — Heel, Come. That lost her points."

Walter stared, then for an agonizing moment he was back at a time when things were always said twice. Because of it he had failed Skeezer. He reached down and rubbed her ears. Learning was always costly. In this case it was points and the dif-

ference between red and blue. He nodded to the judge, then gave the ribbon to Skeezer who took it between her teeth and bounded over the field to give it to the children.

Every hand had to pet her, every one had to praise her, and the same glad commendation was waiting for Walter. Neither one could have done what was done without the other.

"I like red better than blue," Rosey Ann said as she hugged Skeezer.

"It's much more becoming," Tillie said as she fastened the ribbon to Skeezer's collar.

"I guess one is better than two," Walter murmured.

Then a newspaper photographer came up and put a dab of butter on Walter's face. Skeezer started to lick it off. "That'll be my picture of the year," he said as he clicked the camera.

7

Bentley and His Bold Talk

BENTLEY, at eight, had been at CPH longer than any other child. At one time he had been pronounced fit enough to leave, but his home had not proved fit enough to receive him. The tension that had caused his earlier trouble was unresolved and Bentley had returned.

When Bentley was four his mother had walked out of the house and never been heard from again. Bentley remembered her slightly and spoke of her to his psychotherapist in moments of rare confidence, moments that were invariably followed by outbursts of abusive language and violent actions. Bentley's two older brothers in their revolt against their home had been sent to reform school. Bentley's revolt, expressed in rage and aggressiveness, had been thought to be manageable. Considered young enough to be salvaged, psychiatric treatment had been prescribed and he was brought by his father to CPH.

"I'll come every week to see you, Bentley, and I'll bring you a toy," his father said. "You'll have more toys than anyone here."

Bentley stared. His eyes had a glimmer of hope, but his lips were pressed tight together. He knew more about broken promises than ones that were kept.

"Just let him win at games and things," Bentley's father said in an undertone to Miss Williams. "If you don't, you'll have the devil to pay."

Miss Williams was familiar with last minute instructions. They often provided an opportunity to set a parent straight. "Maybe we can help Bentley to lose games, too," she replied.

Nothing was heard from Bentley's father for six months. Even Christmas came without a present. But Skeezer, as she had done for years, was dressed in her Santa Claus costume and went from room to room. The bag that hung around her neck was filled with small packages. In it there was something for everyone. Bentley had a present to open on Christmas day, but he carried within him the hurt of being forgotten.

Under therapy and with the new security felt, Bentley improved. He became more able to control his moments of impulsivity, and though he still liked to win in games, he had discovered that he didn't always have to. At eight, he was ready to be released. His father had recently married again and there was an established home to which he could return. He would be the only child in the household as his brothers were serving prison terms. When his father came for him, Bentley greeted him with a smile of real happiness.

Eighteen months later, Bentley returned to CPH. His stepmother had walked away one day as his natural mother had. His father was incapable of managing him. Some of the children he had known previously were still there, and Skeezer was familiar.

When Bentley arrived, he greeted two of his former friends by hitting them.

"Still got the mutt around," he said, and kicked Skeezer.

There was a scuffle. "You can do anything

you like to me, but you can't hurt Skeezer," Aaron shouted.

Ron got Bentley onto the floor and started pommeling him. Tina and Rosey Ann screamed. Skeezer moved off to a safe distance and watched what was going on.

Strong hands reached into the melee and separated the boys. "That's enough, fellows."

The girls returned to the day room where they had been drawing pictures. The boys sat on the floor facing each other. Bentley, in a voice cautiously lowered, expressed his feelings about life in general and the Sixth Level in particular. His language was fascinating.

"Where'd you learn all those words?"

At first, Bentley didn't want to tell them, then lowering his voice even more, said, "Aw, I belong to a club my brothers started, the DMCC."

"What's that?"

"The Dirty Minded Children's Club. Next time I go home I'll get a lot more words."

"Gee!" Aaron's eyes rolled. "Will you tell them to me?"

"Maybe." Bentley was chary of his wealth.

"That's great."

Aaron stood up. "I'm going to tell Walter."

He started down the hall. "Walter! Walter! Got something to tell you."

"So'm I." Ron ran after him.

Bentley was alone. Skeezer moved over from her place of observation against the wall and pushed herself close to him. Bentley leaned hard against her. She dragged her tongue across his hand. Sure that no one was looking, he put his arm around her and talked to her, telling her the obscenities of which he was so proud. Skeezer didn't care what was said, for the sound of the saying was tender and with his words Bentley proclaimed his love for her. Her tail wagged, her eyes searched the face that was close to hers.

"Don't ever go away, Skeezer, don't ever go away."

Glancing about him to be sure no one could see what he was doing, Bentley put his other arm around her and hugged her. The embrace was too tight for comfort, but Skeezer endured it. "That's the way I used to hug my mom, my real mom, but she went away and left me. And when I hugged my other mom like that she told me to get away."

Bentley found his place as if he had not been away. Past experience served him well. He knew the pattern of the days, and there were other things he knew, too. Even though the furniture was metal, he had learned that by kicking long enough and hard enough, dents could be made in it. Kicking was generally accompanied by yelling and some staff always appeared to impose restraint; sometimes this meant being put in the Quiet Room for a while.

"It's not so bad in there," Bentley boasted to his friends, "and the staff who puts you in always takes you out as soon as you calm down."

The doors at CPH had slam-proof hinges, but Bentley was determined to find a way to overcome that; he was equally determined to find a way to turn off the lights. This gave him a real problem as the switches were operated by keys and all the outlets were controlled from a panel in the nurses' office. But he'd find a way, he told himself and whoever was near to be confided in. Bentley was mad at the world and was ready to fight it out. During his first week he had gone into several rages — once, when Aaron won at a game they were playing. Another time in the dining room when he was not given his plate of food soon enough, he swept his arm across the table and sent everything flying on to the floor.

"Hey," Ron shouted, "we've got rules here!"

Bentley was too blind with rage to see the poster on the wall, or care. A staff picked him up and carried him to the Quiet Room where he could not hurt himself or anyone else.

After a month, a change was noticed. Nurses, child care workers, therapists all agreed that Bentley's frustration tolerance was increasing.

"Half the time I don't know what his words mean," one of the newer staff said to Miss Williams.

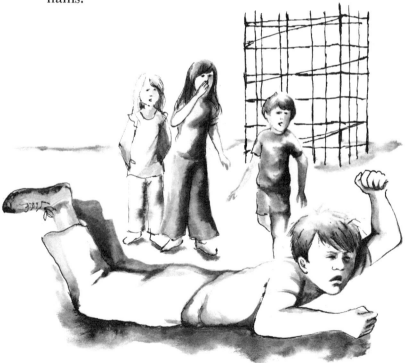

"Neither does Bentley."

"Why would he use that kind of language if he doesn't understand it?"

"Bentley is afraid of close relationships. Using crude, or offensive, language is a way of warding people off."

"Bentley is afraid to love — or be loved?"

"Yes, for love is vulnerability. He's lost out with it twice in his eight years and he can't afford to lose again. I'm glad he has Skeezer."

"He doesn't care about her! Look at the way he kicks her, mauls her. Why, the other day he was found trying to pull out her eyebrows!"

"Love has strange ways," Miss Williams admitted. "Yes, I heard about that from Walter. Bentley told him not to tell, but these children can't keep that kind of secret. They have too many anxieties of their own to stand the added weight of another's guilt."

"It's a wonder Skeezer doesn't turn on him."

"Skeezer won't let anyone mistreat her. She has her way of handling the children. She walks away and her disinterest hurts. It's rarely incurred twice by the same child."

Soon there was general commotion in the hall as the children left their rooms, the day room,

whatever they were doing, for dodge ball in the gymnasium. Skeezer, barking gayly, brought up the rear like a shepherd dog with her flock.

"Maybe Bentley will win tonight."

"Don't count on it," Miss Williams warned.

Soon the Sixth Level was as quiet as it had been noisy. Staff had gone to their various duties and Miss Williams turned to her desk to attend to the many matters that had accumulated on it during the day. But the quiet was soon shattered.

The door at the end of the hall opened and closed quickly. Screams and a rapid fire of words were punctuated by firm footsteps. There was no mistaking the source of the words. The steps were those of one of the male staff.

"You're always blaming me and it was all his fault." The words lost themselves in a high-pitched yell.

"Cool it, Bentley."

"I'll kill him. He's a bitch."

The footsteps went into the day room. Gradually the yells and threats diminished, the voices continued; one loudly abusive, the other gently persuasive. Soon there was comparative quiet. Miss Williams looked up from her desk to face the staff who was standing in her doorway.

"Bentley is upset. When he lost a point it triggered him and he took it out on the nearest boy. He wasn't just slugging, he was biting and kicking. I brought him up to calm him down."

Miss Williams showed no surprise. This was part of any day at CPH. "Bentley can't handle group situations yet when he's under stress. I'll stay with him."

"O.K. I'll go back to the gym."

Bentley was sprawled in a chair sulking when Miss Williams went to him. "How about helping me sort out that box of playing cards in my office?"

"Not for you, you bitch."

"Before you do, Bentley, why don't you go sponge your face off. You'll feel better." Miss Williams went back to her office.

A few moments later water could be heard running. When Bentley appeared in the doorway of the office his shirt was wet, his face clean.

Miss Williams directed his attention to the cards she had begun to sort. "What happened down in the gym, Bentley?"

"I didn't do nothing. It was all Pete's fault. He thinks he's so great because his dad came to see him today." Bentley's fingers trembled as he started to rearrange the cards. "I don't care if my dad never comes to see me. He's a bitch, that's all he is."

"Don't let yourself get so worked up, Bentley."

They sorted the cards into separate piles — spades, hearts, diamonds, clubs.

"Bentley, within the past little while you've called three people a bitch. Do you know what the word means?"

Startled to hear her use a word he had been taught by his brothers was bad, bad, bad, Bentley raised his head. "No."

"A bitch is a female dog."

Bentley stared. He couldn't believe what Miss

Williams was saying, but he had to believe because she was one of the few people he could trust.

"You didn't know that?"

He shook his head. The word was of no use to him any more. It had lost all potency.

Bentley leaned toward Miss Williams and placed a trembling hand on her dress. "You mean," he swallowed hard, "you mean that Skeezer is a bitch?"

"Yes." Miss Williams smiled. Their talk was over. Understanding had been reached between them.

Bentley brushed his hand across his eyes, then he lifted his face to be kissed. All that his hungry heart craved was soon satisfied in the big warm hug that enfolded him.

The door at the end of the hall opened and the children were pouring through it. Laughter and shouts mingled with Skeezer's barks.

"Snack time, Bentley," Miss Williams reminded.

An hour later and the noisy ward stilled. Lights were out except for those in the nurses' office and the staff room, where four of the child care workers were having coffee and writing their observation notes. The only sound was the familiar one of Skeezer's nails clicking on the floor as she made her rounds. At Bentley's door she hesitated. Moving slowly past an obstruction toward his bed, she laid her head on the pillow near his and kept it there.

"Skeezer," he whispered, "Skeezer." He put his arms around her neck, "You old bitch, you."

Skeezer nuzzled him, then turned and went her way.

The night-duty staff arrived and the four who had been on evening duty left. Passing Miss Williams' office they raised their hands in a gesture of leave-taking. Miss Williams often came in late in the morning so she could stay late in the evening to have contact with the night staff. Before leaving, she went down the ward to the boys' end. Skeezer, sleeping in her favorite half-way place, lifted her head and opened her eyes, then went back to sleep.

Miss Williams stood in the doorway of Bentley's room. His steady breathing assured her that he was sleeping so she put on the light. Bentley had placed two chairs just inside his room and strung a rope across them to make a barrier. From the rope hung a notice, crudely lettered on a piece of cardboard, "Everybody except Skeezer, KEEP OUT. I hate you."

She took the rope down and wound it into a coil. Bentley would probably not remember what he had done, or why, when morning came. She stood beside his bed and gazed at the pale face, the hair still damp from a shower, the thin hands that twitched even in sleep.

"The only way to win, Bentley, is to face up to life and take whatever it offers you, the disappointments as well as the victories. You may lose in some things, but you'll come out ahead in the end." She switched out the light and went

down the hall to the staff room.

"Bentley's asleep," she said. "He's all right now."

"That's good."

She opened a drawer for a manila envelope into which she put the piece of rope, then she wrote Bentley's name on it and put it back in the drawer. "I'm going now."

"And we'll be starting our rounds," one of the staff answered. They rose to commence the check of the children, a check that would be repeated every half hour during the night.

Skeezer made no move as they went their separate ways. Her day's work was done.

8

Oriole and the Need for Wings

SHE never should have got into the world, but there she was. Her parents had not even considered names for the child who would have no place in their lives, but the day she was born her mother saw a bright orange bird in the tree outside the hospital window and asked what it was. She was told that it was an oriole.

"That's a pretty name. Let's give it to the baby."

Perhaps the name itself gave the little girl something, for when she was scarcely more than a baby Oriole sang more readily than she talked. As she grew, her slender body looked as if it might fly more easily than walk.

A shiftless father, always looking for the right job and never staying long in any one, an inept mother who clerked intermittently at a dime store but whose main interest was gazing in shop windows at the things she would never have, did nothing to create a home. With little care and less love, the baby grew. Hungry for something, what it was Oriole could not say as she knew only emptiness, she comforted herself with her daydreams.

It was not her father's voice or her mother's that she heard first and frequently, but the cacaphony of the TV put on to drown her infant crying. Noise was all around her, yet when she began to make intelligible sounds and the sounds grew into words, no one listened to them.

At six, when she started to school, something new came into her life and daydreaming diminished. But the contrast with her empty home when she returned from the busy school room was frightening. Climbing the stairs to the shabby apartment on the second floor, unlocking the door with the key that had been given her, she called aloud for her mother. When there was no answer, panic took hold of her. Even though it happened every day, Oriole never seemed able to get used to loneliness.

Hours later, when her parents returned, it was often with a crowd of their friends. There was noise then, loud talk and laughter and rock music. Sometimes they even asked the little girl to sing to them, but the music they made to accompany her drowned out her song.

By the time Oriole was eight she had made up her mind that since she was named for a bird and liked to sing she might even be a bird in disguise. She wanted to fly like a bird so she could fly away from the noise and the bewildering loneliness. She felt sure that she could fly if she became light enough, so she began to eat less. She went close to a month with dwindling interest in food and during that time she became apathetic in school. At recess she chose to sit by herself and do nothing rather than play with the other children.

Her parents were the last to notice how thin she had become, and how listless. Her third grade teacher referred her to the school nurse. Unable to reach her parents, the nurse took Oriole to the doctor. Alarmed by the pencil thin child whose curly hair framed a face in which the eyes were enormous, the doctor gave her a thorough examination and asked that her parents be brought to his office.

When her mother was finally reached and advised by the doctor of her child's condition, she exclaimed in exasperation, "But there's food in the refrigerator! All Oriole needed to do was help herself. I don't know why she hasn't been eating."

The doctor explained that a growing child needed more than food.

"Can't we force something down her to get her over being so stubborn?"

"Force feeding can be resorted to only as an emergency measure. It does no long term good. Your child is profoundly depressed."

"Depressed?"

He nodded.

"What's that?"

"Depression is a defense mechanism not a disease in itself. It is a symptom of an emotional problem, sometimes a sadness so deep that special help is required to recover from it."

"And you're talking about Oriole?"

"Yes." The doctor chose his words carefully. "It would be well for your child to have psychiatric treatment as soon as it can conveniently be arranged."

Far from being perturbed, Oriole's parents saw the diagnosis and eventual prescription as a way of having their lives freed from the impediment of a child.

Oriole arrived at CPH in the care of the school nurse.

Some of the children came to stand in the hall and stare at her, offering friendship wordlessly. Others remained before the TV in the day room, watching a favorite program.

"I don't like noise," Oriole said and looked up at Miss Williams.

"Don't you?"

Oriole shook her head. Deliberately she walked across the room and turned off the television set.

"Oh!" the school nurse exclaimed. "Won't the children mind?"

"Probably not this first time," Miss Williams said. "Oriole is new and they're curious. That's generally enough to make them tolerant. By tomorrow she may be watching television with them."

No matter what Skeezer was doing or where her calls throughout the building took her, she managed to make an appearance when a new arrival came. When Oriole was shown her room, Skeezer followed her into it and moved up to stand between the little girl and Miss Williams. Reaching toward her, Skeezer pushed her nose into the small bony hand. Then she barked questioningly.

Oriole looked at her. This was the first time a dog had come into her life and she wasn't sure what to do. She moved away from Skeezer and stood behind a chair. "What does she want?" she asked Miss Williams.

"She wants to be your friend," was the comforting answer.

Skeezer sat down on her haunches and waited. Oriole reached out her hand cautiously.

That was the night of the Halloween party. After supper, instead of going down to the gym for games, they had them on the Sixth Level. Children disappeared into their rooms to put on their costumes, then emerged to mystify themselves and each other as spooks and goblins. Skeezer came out of the nurses' office wearing a black cloak over her shoulders. A tall peaked hat that was tied under her chin slipped around her head every time her ears moved. A small white ghost cut from stiff paper rode on her back.

"Here comes the witch!" the children shrieked and raced down the hall, then turned and ran back again to crowd around her.

"You can't fool me," Rosey Ann said. "I know who you are."

Skeezer stood before them, ears moving forward then back, stub tail wagging, knowing she was the center of attention and relishing it.

Jessie dashed off to her room to get a camera. Ron appeared with a pad and some crayons and started to draw a picture of Skeezer. Walter placed his hand on her back to keep her still, though she had no intention of moving. When the pose had been held long enough to suit everyone's purpose, Bentley closed his fingers around her tail and said, "Now you're wound up to go." He gave Skeezer a push that dislodged the white ghost and toppled the hat so it slid between her front legs and hung there dangling until a staff removed it.

The children's voices were shrill and gay as they danced around their dog. Skeezer looked as if she was having the most fun of all.

"She may be only one-third Doberman," one of the staff said, "but she's got the breed's ability to clown; doesn't mind being laughed at either."

After the games it was snack time, cookies shaped and colored like pumpkins, apples, candy. Even Skeezer was allowed a share for Halloween came only once a year and she had earned her treat. Oriole found that one cookie was so good she took another. The noise and merrymaking ceased while they were eating and Oriole saw her moment.

"I'm going to sing you a song," she announced.

They listened and applauded when she came to the end.

Oriole smiled and made a little bow. Happiness had begun to sing in her like another kind of song.

The latch-key child, once so fearful of the emptiness around her that she had had to fill it with phantasying, responded to the life at CPH. The many sounds through the day were comforting for they meant people — clatter in the kitchen, doors opening and closing, telephones ringing. Sitting down on the floor beside Skeezer wherever she came upon her, Oriole would press her lips close to one of the flopped-over ears. "Listen and I'll tell you a story." Then in a voice that was whisper low she told Skeezer about a new kind of bird who was finding wings with which to fly.

The marvel to Oriole was that Skeezer was always ready to listen. Whenever she returned to the Sixth Level from school, or an afternoon of outdoor play, or an hour in the pool, Skeezer was there as if waiting for her. Sometimes she was lazy and wanted to go on sleeping, then Oriole sat beside her and sang in her reedy little voice. Often Skeezer twitched as if she were dreaming and the involuntary movements forged tighter the link between them, for Oriole remembered that dreams, waking dreams, had once been her only escape.

Invariably, sleeping or awake, a time would come when Skeezer thumped her stub tail on the floor, stirred herself to lick Oriole's hand and gazed at her with an expression that told Oriole all she needed to know.

Oriole's psychotherapist, talking one day with Miss Williams, said, "Often I don't have to do anything but let her talk. It's as if no one had ever listened to her."

"No one did, except in school."

"I just say *m-m-m,* or make some small sounds."

Miss Williams repeated, "*M-m-m,* that's sometimes the most therapeutic thing one can say. It means 'I'm listening.' "

The Sixth Level children were on their way down to the pool and Skeezer watched them go, standing aside as they went past her. Like the dining room, the pool was a place where she did not go. But she generally made good use of her time while the children were away and visited one or another of the levels. Her calls throughout the building were such a matter of course that no one took any notice of her comings and goings.

"Skeezer!" Oriole called on returning from the pool, hair damp, eyes shining with the fun had in the warm water.

If Skeezer was asleep on one of the beds, or under a desk in the nurses' office, it took her a little while to make an appearance. Oriole waited patiently, expectantly, then she called again, "Skeezer!"

When there was no answering appearance, Oriole ran through the hall, looking in one room after another, and calling beseechingly.

Panic seized her. Her voice became high and sharp as she continued to look, continued to call Skeezer's name. Her life had been empty for so long, filled for so short a time, that the past overcame her. The fear that had gripped her when she let herself into the apartment with her latchkey and called her mother's name gripped her again.

"Skeezer's not here," she wailed to the children in the day room.

"She's just making one of her calls," Walter said, "she'll be back soon."

The fact that there were people to talk to calmed Oriole. She went to the nurses' office. "Where's Skeezer?"

"Probably at one of the other levels," Miss Williams answered.

"But she's always here when I get back and she's. . . ."

Miss Williams picked up the phone and called the Third Level, asking for Skeezer. She called the Fourth and Fifth Levels with the same question, then she turned back to Oriole. "Skeezer has visited each one of the levels today, but her calls were made this morning. If she were in the elevator you would have met her on your way up from the pool. Let's try the front desk."

By now, a group of children had collected in the doorway and were standing behind Oriole.

Miss Williams received the information she was seeking and relayed it to them. "About an hour ago, someone at the desk saw Skeezer going out behind a visitor as if being taken for a walk. She looked as if she knew what she was doing."

"Skeezer always knows what she's doing," Walter said.

"But where is she?" One after another the children took up Oriole's question. Their eyes went toward the window. It was too high to see anything but sky. Somewhere below was the campus of the Medical School with more streets than lawns. Traffic was heavy and it moved swiftly, especially in the late afternoon.

"Skeezer is lost," Miss Williams explained to the children. "I'm going out to find her." She took her car keys from the drawer and Skeezer's lead from a hook on the wall.

Oriole hugged her arms around her thin body. The ward without Skeezer was an empty place, no matter who else was in it. "If I were a bird. . . ." she began.

It was soon time for supper. Oriole pushed away her food untouched.

Tillie said, "I'm so worried. I'm worried about everything."

Ron said, "When our dog was lost he was never found."

Poppy's voice quavered, "I knew a dog who ran away and was killed by a truck."

One after another they told of things they

knew had happened to their own or to other's pets; and when they didn't actually know they invented a happening.

When Miss Williams returned they looked toward her hopefully, but the lead swung loose in her hand. "We've put an ad in the paper," she said, "and I'll go out again tomorrow."

"Well, I guess that's the end of Skeezer." Bentley tried to sound as if he didn't care.

Doom had descended upon them all, no matter how they sought to disguise it.

Miss Williams went out in her car the next day, up one street, down another, whistling the few notes that had always brought Skeezer to her. She passed several fraternity houses and as she drove by, waves and answering whistles from boys sitting on the steps greeted her. It was not until the third day that the search was rewarded. Driving slowly through a residential street, Miss Williams caught sight of Skeezer sitting on a lawn surrounded by dogs. She stopped the car, opened the front door and whistled. Exasperation that had become genuine anxiety were both dissolved in relief.

Skeezer alerted and stood up. Then, without so much as a look around or a backward glance, she bounded toward the car, jumped in and took her place on the front seat.

Back at CPH, when Miss Williams unsnapped the lead from Skeezer's collar, Skeezer raced down the hall barking, greeting and greeted by her friends.

"SKEEZER!" they shouted.

She went from child to child, tail wagging, body wriggling, giving more kisses than she received, so glad she was to be back with them. No one asked her any questions; most of them knew how impossible it was to explain behavior.

"I think she decided that she needed a vacation," Miss Williams said, "and the only way she could get one was to take it herself. She's been on duty for quite a long time."

So it was settled that Skeezer should have a weekend off now and then, just as the children did when they went home with their parents. Her time would be spent in the country with one of the staff whose parents had a farm.

"Anyone needs a break," Aaron added with feeling.

"I won't mind when she's not here," Oriole said, "because I'll know where she is."

That night, when lights were out and Skeezer

made her rounds, she spent a little more time than usual with each child as if to make up for the time she had missed when away.

Oriole was singing softly to herself when Skeezer got to her room. Skeezer placed her head on the blanket and watched Oriole. She looked as if she would stay there as long as the song lasted or as long as Oriole wanted her.

When Oriole stopped singing she flung her arms around Skeezer and put her nose close to Skeezer's. "Oh, I'm so glad you're a dog, Skeezer!"

Skeezer licked her face.

"You're tickling me, Skeezer, but I like to be tickled."

When Skeezer left and went on to the next room, Oriole laughed. What she had just said struck her as very funny. How could Skeezer possibly be anything but what she was. A dog was a dog. Oriole, snuggling back on the pillow, was ready to go further and admit to herself that a little girl was a little girl and a bird was a bird.

"And that's all there is to that," she said to herself in the darkness.

9

Willie John. What's Big?

IT was a rainy day. The children were having games in the day room and the hall. Skeezer had been dressed in a white coat, an old stethoscope had been hung round her neck and she was answering calls for Dr. Skeezer. Far more important to her than the stethoscope was the small pouch she carried around her neck, for it contained balloons. Ron had congested ear canals and the pediatrician had suggested that he gently blow up balloons every few hours.

Skeezer delivered the balloons, not only to Ron but to the other children. Soon balloons were being blown up all over the ward. Floating high and low, Skeezer jumped for every one that came near her. In spite of the equipment she carried and her white coat, she managed to catch and puncture several.

When the door at the end of the hall opened, the children stopped their play to see who was coming through it. At the sight of a boy new to them, they moved toward the door to see him more closely. Skeezer ambled back to the office for one of the nurses to remove her costume.

"Hello, Willie-John," Miss Williams addressed the stormy looking boy who stood between a man and a woman, each holding one of his hands. "Your friends are here to welcome you."

Willie-John paid no attention to Miss Williams or to the children lining up along the wall. He saw only one thing and it was what he wanted. Pulling his hands free and letting out a muffled sound, he ran down the hall to Skeezer's house. Flinging himself down, he crawled into it.

"That's all he ever wants to do since it happened," the woman, a staff member from the local crisis clinic, said, "Hide."

"Or swagger," the man, who was a social worker, added. "If you don't let him stay there until he decides to come out, he'll bust it up for

good, then tell you how big he is. That's all he talks about — busting things up."

"Won't the dog object when Willie-John is found in its house?" the woman asked guardedly. "Willie-John doesn't get on with dogs. They snap at him."

"He teases them, that's why."

"No," Miss Williams started to lead the way to her office. "Skeezer doesn't mind who uses her house."

The children drifted off, some to the day room, others to their own rooms. Nobody paid any particular attention to the new arrival. Skeezer came out of the nurses' office and went toward her house. She nosed the pair of short sturdy legs that were protruding, the shoes that had no familiar smell. She ran her nose as far as it would go, snuffling, then she squeezed herself into and through the opening. Flattening herself down, she pressed her back against one side to make the small place big enough for two.

Rosey Ann, passing down the hall, saw what was happening and reported it back to the day room. "Skeezer's got a new friend."

Bentley, more aware of numbers than some

of the others, said, "That makes twelve of us now on the Sixth Level."

When the two who had accompanied Willie-John left, Miss Williams went with them to the door. As they passed 866 Puppy Lane, they could see that Willie-John's position had changed hardly at all except that his legs were drawn in more closely. The social worker started toward the elevator, relieved to have Willie-John in safe hands.

"Such a nice boy, really, so bright," the woman hesitated. "But since it happened. . . ." her voice trailed away.

"He can be helped," Miss Williams said with quiet assurance.

When Skeezer was called to her supper, she emerged from her house followed by a rumpled looking boy. A staff, standing near, greeted Willie-John and showed him around the ward, then took him to his room and helped him get settled. When the children were called to the dining room, Willie-John took his place at a table with three other boys and discovered that he was hungry.

It was late that evening when Miss Williams talked with the two night duty nurses about the new arrival. "Since it happened," she began. The words, used twice that afternoon, were like a title to Willie-John's story. Miss Williams and other members of the staff were familiar with it since the boy's pre-admission visit three months before. They had discussed it as they prepared for his arrival at CPH. The night staff had not been a part of the earlier discussions and Miss Williams wanted to bring them up to date.

No one knew how it had happened, no one was to blame, but Willie-John would carry its memory through life.

Willie-John and his sister Polly, younger by a year, had been playing together with an electric train when some safeguard failed and the little girl was electrocuted. During the weeks that followed, Willie-John's feeling of guilt grew so that it became insupportable; it took itself out in ways that were incomprehensible to the adults who made up his world. During those weeks he had never been seen to cry; that he had not laughed or smiled went unnoticed.

Outwardly defiant, inwardly sick with guilt, he resented sympathy. He flinched from his mother's arms, stood his ground during his father's outbursts of anger, then skulked away to hide. His first recourse was a clumsy attempt at suicide. This had enraged his father so that he beat him. Overcome by remorse, his father then tried to make up to Willie-John by buying a horse for him.

Willie-John wouldn't go near the horse.

His father tried again, sold the horse and brought home a dog as big as a pony.

Willie-John ran from it and refused to enter the house as long as the dog was there.

"But why?" his mother asked. "You're always talking about how big you are. Why don't you like big things?"

Willie-John resisted reasoning as he did any show of tenderness. With his friends he boasted of his bigness, swaggered before them, bullied those he could, and told them he was going to lick the world but that he'd bust it up first. At night, when no one could see him, he shook with his own fear and often got out of his bed to sleep under it. His guilt was a giant stalking him, waiting to bear down on him. The only way he could hold the giant off was to do things that would show others how big and powerful he was.

One day he smashed to bits the electric train and everything that went with it. That might be understandable, but not the destruction of his little sister's dolls.

"Why, Willie-John, why did you do it?"

There was no answer, only a puckering of lips, a folding of his arms across his chest, and a stamping of his feet even more solidly upon the ground.

His mother, doubly grief-stricken, pleaded with him. "If you were really sorry for what happened to Polly you would try to be a help to us instead of doing these dreadful things."

"You can't get me," Willie-John retorted. "I'm big, nobody's going to get me."

"Nobody's trying to get you," his father said, "we're just asking you to be sensible."

Willie-John scowled and pressed his lips so tightly together that the color drained from them. Communication on any count, for any reason, did not exist. Willie-John was at war with his world, and with himself.

One day at school, during recess, he broke several windows and attempted to choke another boy. It was then that the school authorities turned to the crisis clinic. Medical consultation followed. Psychiatric treatment was recommended. In the course of time Willie-John arrived at CPH and his first move was to take refuge in Skeezer's house.

He soon fitted into the new life, going on with his school work, doing constructive projects in O.T., responding to the thrice weekly hours with

his psychotherapist. His war on the world sur-
rendered to the peaceful pattern at CPH.

On afternoon bike rides or hikes in the nearby
park, Skeezer generally ran free. The children
liked to throw sticks in the river for her to retrieve.
Sometimes Walter called her to him and put her
through the commands they had learned together
in Obedience Class. Bentley liked to get her on her
lead, then try to make her pull him. On one such
outing, Bentley had just snapped the lead to her
collar when Skeezer saw a rabbit. Almost before
anyone knew what had happened, Skeezer dashed
away after the rabbit with the lead dangling.

"I'll get her," Willie-John shouted and ran
in pursuit.

But it wasn't all that easy. Skeezer on the
loose with a rabbit to chase was another dog.
Willie-John raced up a sandhill and followed her
into the brush before he caught up with her.

Back on the Sixth Level, when he related the
incident to Miss Williams, he was elated. "Guess
who caught Skeezer? Good old Me! I was the only
one who volunteered to go into the pricker bushes
after her."

Willie-John had been at CPH a month when

his parents came to see him. His father brought him a watch. The band was too big for the boy's wrist and when the watch slipped off and onto the floor Willie-John stared at it for a moment. Then he let out a cry of rage and stamped on the watch. Before he could be stopped it was shattered beyond repair.

"Why?" said Willie-John's mother.

His father made his hands into fists to hold back his anger.

They left soon after and when the door closed behind them Willie-John kicked it until he was restrained. The door was accustomed to rough treatment, the boy's shoes were not.

"They always give me things that are too big," Willie-John sobbed, "but I'll show them what's big."

He went down to the day room and flung himself on the couch. Skeezer was already there but she moved over to make room.

Oriole, standing near, said, "Nobody ever comes to see me and bring me presents, even on my birthday. A watch too big would be better than no watch at all."

"Oh, you think you know everything," Willie-John muttered, then he lunged out with one of his legs to kick Oriole away.

She dodged neatly and all Willie-John accomplished was to displace Skeezer. Landing on the floor, she shook herself, then without so much as a backward look, walked sedately away.

Willie-John thumped his hands against the couch and buried his head under a pillow. He was back in the time when everyone was against him — kids who teased him, teachers who were hard on him, parents who scolded him. "I'll show them all, I'll bust up everything and show them." Then he threw the pillow across the room and got up to follow Skeezer.

Finding her, he sat down on the floor beside her and began rolling some gum between his fingers. "I'll even show you, Skeezer." He pushed her to make her lie over on one side. Taking hold of a front paw, he started to move back the hair from around the pads so he could put gum in between. "I'm going to fix you so you'll stick to the floor and won't be able to move when anyone calls you. How'll you like that?"

Skeezer enjoyed conversation, and though her vocabulary contained a score of words whose meaning was clearly understood, not one of them was being used by Willie-John. She was not being asked to sit or stay or fetch, a walk was not being suggested or a ride or a ball game; but she was being made a confidante. The low voice, the head bent near, the hand holding her paw, all said as much.

The most ticklish place for a dog is the area between the pads of its feet and as Willie-John pushed the hair back, Skeezer drew her paw away quickly. She stood up and shook herself.

"No you won't," Willie-John said, putting the gum in his mouth and grabbing her forelegs with both hands.

The tone of voice had changed, so had the motions, as the easily angered boy mauled the dog and tried to drag her down to the floor. This was no friendly tussle and Skeezer knew it. She merely did what she had often done before when a child's play took on another proportion, what her ancestors had been trained to do when tracking criminals. She rolled Willie-John onto his back, put her forepaws on his chest and held him there until someone saw her.

"All right, Skeezer," a staff called from down the hall.

Skeezer got up and walked away with dignity. Turning into the nurses' office, she went under one of the desks.

"Come on, Willie-John," staff said, "it's time for O.T., some of the kids have already gone down."

Willie-John stood up slowly. "It was all Skeezer's fault, she—" but he found he couldn't vent the blame and still keep gum in his mouth.

The next day he found a place for the gum in the locks of certain of the doors. "Now they'll know who's the biggest."

Triumph was hollow and short-lived. The act was soon discovered. The locks were freed as the gum was removed with cleaning fluid. No one asked who did it, or why, and life went on at CPH.

Willie-John sat in the day room when the children went trooping down the hall on one of their evening visits to the store.

"Aren't you coming?" one of them called.

He shook his head. He didn't know what he wanted to do except that he didn't want to be with them. He felt in his pocket. Two nickels were there. That would have been enough to buy a candy bar. He began to wish he had gone with them, but it was too late now. The door was closed.

By the time the children got back, Willie-John was standing in the hall waiting for them. Skeezer stood beside him.

"Look, Skeezer, I've got some balloons for you!" cried Aaron, holding a limp bit of bright blue rubber to his mouth. He blew it up until it was the size of a basketball.

Skeezer quivered with eagerness for her moment. The balloon was held high, then tossed into the air. She jumped for it but missed. It was tossed to another child who caught it. Skeezer jumped again and on the third try brought it down. It slipped away from her paws and bounced down the hall. Skeezer went after it while half a dozen children raced after her, laughing and shouting as they called her name.

This time the balloon was caught, and with one swift downward movement of paws burst into nothingness.

Willie-John watched, waiting to hear Skeezer
rebuked for her destructiveness, or asked "Why?"

The remnant of balloon on the floor was ig-
nored by everyone.

"Wait a minute, Skeezer, "I've got another
one for you."

And so it went, until six balloons bought for

a nickel had been blown up, tossed high, chased, finally demolished, and Skeezer was praised for her prowess.

"Doesn't it matter if she busts those balloons?" Willie-John asked.

" 'Course not! It's her game. We always bring some back for her when we go to the store."

Willie-John stared: so some things were made to be busted.

"Want to try one with her?"

"Sure." Willie-John accepted a bright red bit of rubber, put it gingerly to his mouth and started to blow into it. When his breath gave out he stopped.

"That's not big enough. Keep blowing."

Tight-mouthed and red-faced he blew and the balloon grew until it was its full size.

"Now, I'll show you how to keep the air in it," Walter said as he twisted the rubber at the end.

Skeezer, her eyes on the balloon, stood poised to follow its course. Her mouth was open, she was panting with excitement.

"It has to be big enough to be fun," Walter explained, "but not so big that it bursts before Skeezer has her fun."

Rosey Ann's parents had arrived to take her

home for the weekend. Rosey Ann came running up to Skeezer to pet her. "So you'll know I'm coming back." She put her nose close to Skeezer, "And when I come back on Sunday night you'll say hello to me the way I'm saying good-by to you." Then she skipped away to join her parents at the door.

Willie-John watched her. "Maybe my parents will come some day for me."

"Could be," Aaron said and handed Willie-John another balloon.

It was blown up, tossed in the air, and Skeezer leaped for it. She missed. Aaron batted it to Willie-John who batted it to Walter. Down the hall the balloon went, kept in the air by many deft hands. Running feet pursued Skeezer as she pursued the balloon. Finally, in one of her leaps, she brought it down, held it between her paws for a second of triumph, then punctured it with her teeth. The children laughed and clapped their hands.

"That was big!" Willie-John laughed with them.

"I'll say it was."

"That was really big. Let's blow up another."

10

Gwen and Length of Days

THE children were not often discomfited by anything outside themselves. It was their own turmoil, the conflicts within, that upset them, caused them to forfeit hard-won control and made them want to hide, scream, break things. Their hold on reality was still fragile, and Gwen broke it.

She looked like a little shapeless woman when her parents brought her to the Sixth Level. There were deep circles under her eyes and her eyes were vague, as if she didn't see what she was staring at. Her skin was without color, the lines of her face went down. But she was a child like them, not nearly so tall as Aaron or so rounded as Jessie; her hands were small. She was nicely dressed and her hair was neatly combed, but she looked like an old person dressed up as a child.

"This is Gwen Barrett," Miss Williams said to the children.

Gwen said nothing. Months ago, she had lost the power to speak.

Some of the children were standing in the doorway of the day room, others were leaning against the wall in the hall. The curious turned away; those ready to be friendly abandoned their impulse. Two or three went back to whatever they had been doing; several sought their own rooms and threw themselves down on their beds, fingers tense, feet kicking spasmodically as if to drive away something that was as unknown as it was unwanted.

Skeezer, who had been standing with the children, did not drop her gaze, did not move away, but remained in the middle of the hall; four feet planted firmly, head raised questioningly, short tail poised.

"That's Skeezer," Miss Williams said. "She'd like to make friends with you, Gwen."

The child's parents kissed her good-by and left. Everything that needed to be done and said had been taken care of on their earlier visits.

"It will soon be time for supper, Gwen, and Skeezer does not come in to the dining room. You may stay with her if you wish." Miss Williams went to her office.

Soon there was no one in the hall but the child and the dog.

Skeezer waited.

Gwen took one step forward and held out her hand; then she took another step.

Toward the child enclosed in silence moved the dog who had no speech. Gwen knelt and put her arms around Skeezer. Their eyes were on a level. With all the hunger and hurt that had been locked within her for so long, Gwen searched Skeezer's eyes.

Skeezer dropped to her haunches. Gwen sat down, drawing her legs under her awkward body. A bell sounded from the dining room. Children left their pursuits or their aimlessness to answer it. None of them took any notice of the two crouched on the floor in the middle of the hall.

Gwen put her nose against Skeezer's and felt the dog's warm breath on her face. She blew gently and the dog's ears moved back, then forward. Gwen's fingers felt their way through the deep coat and came to rest on the broad chest. She rubbed it. Skeezer sniffed Gwen's ears, then pushed her muzzle against Gwen's cheek. Gwen shifted her position to be more comfortable and ran her hand down Skeezer's back. Skeezer placed a front paw on Gwen's knee, then drew her tongue across the child's hand. Eyes looked into eyes, each pleading: one for the love needed, the other with love to give. Gwen's lips trembled into a smile. Skeezer's tail quivered.

Long before speech existed, feelings had been communicated by intensity of need. The child and the dog were back in that time together. Their language was silent, but each understood the other.

By the end of the first week, Gwen wrote a letter home. She asked her parents to send her a snapshot of her dog. "I want to show it to Skeezer." Written words were the first break in her long muteness.

From time to time Miss Williams talked with her staff about the children. Each one was particular; Gwen no more no less than any other. "She was a healthy happy little girl with parents who cherished her," Miss Williams said. "Her father used to call her the apple of his eye."

"Used to?"

Miss Williams nodded, indicating that much of Gwen's story was wrapped up in those two words.

Gwen had a dog of her own, a pony, playmates nearby, a lovely home in the country, but when she was ten she began to evidence all the symptoms of leukemia. What vulnerability, what exposure, had made one healthy child in a healthy community the victim of a debilitating disease was a mystery. The local doctor did his best, but after several weeks Gwen was taken to the pediatric unit of University Hospital at Ann Arbor. Medication helped arrest the course of the leukemia, but her constitution had been so weakened that the potent drugs had severe side effects. Her parents called for her when she was considered well enough to go home. They were shocked by her appearance. She was heavy and bloated; she looked as if she had aged half a lifetime.

The doctors told the Barretts it was unlikely that Gwen would grow to womanhood, but that with medication she might be able to enjoy a few years of limited health. Without medication, even though it had disagreeable side effects, little hope could be given. The Barretts made their decision, hard as it might be: care at home and periodic returns to the hospital. Gwen was their child, their only one, and as long as life lasted they wanted to do all that could be done for her.

No one knew why it was that Gwen took matters into her own hands. On the long drive home, she was apparently sleeping on the back seat of the car and her parents were talking together. They heard a shuffling sound, felt a rush of cold air, and turned to see Gwen half way out the rear window. Mrs. Barrett flung herself across the back of the seat and grabbed her daughter's ankles. Mr. Barrett pulled off to the service strip and braked, then he leaped out and held on to Gwen as cars rushed by.

"I want to die," Gwen sobbed as her parents got her back in the car. They were the last words they heard her speak.

Gwen was hysterical so Mrs. Barrett stayed with her on the back seat until they reached home. Once in the house, Gwen ran and locked herself in the bathroom. Neither entreaty nor threat could get her out, only the removal of the door.

The weeks and months that followed were a nightmare to the Barretts; what they were to Gwen no one knew as she had lost all power to communicate. It was not that she wouldn't talk but that she couldn't. Medical advice was to include psychiatric treatment along with the drugs she was being given for the leukemia.

So she came to CPH where time was measured in ways other than by clocks and calendars.

Gwen's silent conversations with Skeezer began to include whisperings, then croonings. If anyone heard or observed, nothing in particular was said; but the morning Gwen asked at breakfast for someone to please pass her the sugar was a day to be noted. The children did not seem surprised at the sound of her voice, but they were by her politeness, especially those for whom manners were something new. Gwen then began to talk with her psychotherapist. She had a preoccupation with death, and what she had once sought on the highway had become what she most feared.

Skeezer was still the one with whom she could freely share her worries.

"Oh, Skeezer," she confided, "Mama and Papa were talking about me that night when we were all on our way home. They thought I was asleep, but I heard them. They said they couldn't bear to look at me, that I looked like my grandmother. Oh, Skeezer, I don't look that awful to you, do I? Do I?"

Skeezer's eyes searched Gwen's face. She reached her nose toward it and let Gwen feel the tip of her tongue.

"Skeezer, they said I used to be pretty, but—" and then, for all the self control Gwen had been gaining, she couldn't hold back the tears, "They said not many people would see me. Oh, Skeezer, you think I'm still pretty, don't you?"

Skeezer flattened out on her side and sighed. Low tones directed only to her filled her with bliss. She closed her eyes.

Steps could be heard in the hall. Gwen brushed her hand across her face and looked up to see Miss Williams.

"Something special coming up next week, Gwen."

Gwen's smile, usually wistful, was radiant. "Next week's my birthday."

"So it is, and we're all going to Dexter-Huron Park for a cookout."

"Skeezer, too?"

"Of course."

Gwen dropped her eyes for a moment. "When people ask me my age I say thirteen, because I shall be soon."

Skeezer was in high spirits, as were the children, the day they climbed into the three station wagons and went to the park. Skeezer's spirits were, perhaps, a little higher than usual, for Miss Williams, the one to whom she owed complete attention, was not going with them. Skeezer could be known to take advantage of or use to her own advantage other staff, but never Miss Williams.

The children played games, climbed trees, ran races, like any merry crowd of noisy happy youngsters. Supervision, casual in appearance, was ever present. Two nurses and four child care workers were also enjoying the fun, but alert for the moment when play might become unruly and some diversion was required.

Skeezer dashed into the water to retrieve sticks thrown for her. When she came out and shook herself, the children standing near had all the advantage of a shower on a hot day.

"Here, Skeezer, here," they called, luring her to them.

Once Willie-John got the most. "That's cool, Skeezer, fast little drops made by you are better than the shower at CPH."

Skeezer ran from rock to rock in the stream, then pounced on a sock to retrieve it. Nosing it carefully, she decided that it belonged to Oriole and went leaping off to find her. But she had no intention of giving it to Oriole, merely showing it as invitation to a game. If Oriole wanted it, she would have to catch Skeezer first. When Oriole finally caught her, Skeezer opened her mouth and the sock fell to the ground.

While the children were having their cookout, Skeezer went off on her own. When she returned, she had a freshly killed young raccoon between her jaws. True to her retrieving instinct, she laid it at the feet of one of the staff. The mood of the day changed. Noisy voices became quiet. The children were shocked and perplexed. No one said "Bad dog," but no one praised her; nor did they try to explain the situation away by saying that perhaps she had found the raccoon and was only doing what a good Labrador should in bringing it to them. They were no more inclined to excuse her than themselves in a fault. The evidence was before them and it spoke for itself.

Gwen broke the silence and asked if they could bury the raccoon in some pretty place. This gave release. Now a group of mourners, the children attended the ceremony and among them no one was more decorous than Skeezer. Gwen sat down by the mound of newly-turned earth and the children started back to their play. None of them called to Skeezer to join them; one or two brushed her away when she went up to them. Her ears drooped, her tail sagged, and she turned to look at Gwen.

Gwen snapped her fingers. Skeezer moved toward her. Everything about Skeezer's attitude said that this time she needed Gwen. The two sat close together.

Without Skeezer the games had lost much of their fun, and gradually the children drifted back to sit beside Gwen. Skeezer was there, her head resting against Gwen's knee, her eyes were open.

"What you doing?" Rosey Ann asked.

"Thinking," Gwen replied, as if her thirteen years gave her the right to such a statement. "Skeezer and I have been telling each other things."

"What kind of things?"

"About dogs and raccoons."

The eyes fixed on Gwen looked wondering.

"You see," Gwen said, choosing her words carefully, "animals live when they're living. They don't bother about anything except what's happening right now. They just are and they just do. And that's why they're not afraid."

"How come you know all this?" Bentley asked.

"Skeezer told me."

When the station wagons went back to CPH, Gwen sat on the front seat of one with Skeezer beside her. They seemed at peace in each other's company, as if something had been settled between them.

Back on the Sixth Level, Gwen changed into a clean dress, combed her hair and got ready for supper; then she went down the hall to Miss Williams' office. She had something to say and she knew to whom she wanted to say it. She stood quietly in the doorway until Miss Williams asked her to come in and motioned to the chair near her desk.

Gwen sat down, smoothed her dress and folded her hands in her lap. "Skeezer says I'm the apple of her eye."

Miss Williams looked long and lovingly at Gwen. "That's fine, Gwen, that's just fine."

Gwen smiled.

Miss Williams nodded as if to underscore what she had said. Gwen would soon be leaving CPH, but during her time she had become able to speak, to play with children, to accept life as it was for her and would be. The event that had happened in the park had been an unusual kind of birthday present since it had freed Gwen from a deeply lodged fear.

"I'm glad, Gwen, and glad you told me."

Gwen eased herself from the chair and left the room.

11

Home for Good

AFTER two months at CPH, Willie-John had
his weekend at home. When he returned from it,
early on a Sunday evening, he was brim full with
his news. Skeezer was standing in the hall and
Willie-John ran to her. He flung himself down on
the floor to put his arms around her more easily.

"Skeezer," he said, in a voice shrill with excitement, "they gave me a dog! My folks gave me
a dog! Her name is Gretchen and she looks just
like you."

Skeezer moved her ears conversationally, her
tail jigged.

"Everytime I go home she'll be there to say

hello to me the way you do here."

Aaron, standing near, asked what kind of a dog.

"Gretchen is a Dachshund," Willie-John said with pride.

"And she looks like Skeezer?"Aaron exploded. "Man, you need a pair of eyeglasses!"

Willie-John studied Skeezer for a moment. "Well," he said, "their noses are alike."

Aaron went to find Bentley to relay the news to him.

Willie-John scratched the place between Skeezer's ears. "I know you love me, Skeezer, but you better understand now that my dog loves me just a little bit more."

Skeezer licked the face that was close to hers.

Willie-John was relieved that she understood. He got up and went to the day room to see who was there.

Bentley was there, writing a letter to his Seventh Grade teacher. "In regard to our dog Skeezer, I could state the obvious," he read aloud to any who cared to listen, "just mentioning things like her riding in the elevator on her own. Those things by themselves seem tremendous but are really trifles when you know Skeezer. She doesn't

care about those things really. It's hard to explain but she lives her own life like you, me, or anyone. She lets on that she's superior but she really likes to be babied and played with. We all like her that way."

Poppy was sitting on the vinyl-covered couch. At sight of her Skeezer jumped up to sit beside her. When Poppy came to CPH she had never been close to a dog in her life and Skeezer had bewildered her. "Is the dog sick, too?" she had asked. "Is that why the dog is in the hospital?"

"No," Miss Williams had said, "Skeezer is here for the children. She's your friend."

When Poppy wrote her first letter home she had said in it, "Remember that dog I was scared of? I stopped being scared because she liked me. I took her out on her lead and we ran together. She chased me and I chased her. It wouldn't be much fun here without Skeezer."

Writing was hard for Rosey Ann. It took her a long time to make letters on a large piece of paper, and sometimes she was the only one who could read them. With help from a staff, she finally got down on paper something she wanted her parents to know, "If Skeezer were here and I wasn't, she'd be pretty sad."

Each child who came to CPH came with a different need. Gwen's had been for someone with whom she could share the silence that had engulfed her, Oriole's for someone to listen to her plaintive whisperings. Willie-John needed someone to be rough with. In games he played, especially those outdoors, Skeezer was more than a match for him. He never could get the better of her, but when she felt that a race or a roughhouse had gone long enough, she was the one to call quits. Lying down and panting, her long tongue lolled out of her mouth. Willie-John, physically tired and temporarily free of inner pressure, threw himself down beside her. Skeezer, unless she was being mistreated, could be counted on to stay indefinitely.

Tillie, frail and asthmatic, had been fussed

over so much of her young life that she needed to fuss over someone herself. Skeezer never minded how many bows Tillie tied around her neck or her tail, never minded how often Tillie propped pillows under her head or her paws when she was asleep.

Cindy, growing up lonely and alone in a house of elderly relatives, needed a playmate. Skeezer soon assured her that she had just that. Cindy shared one of the double rooms with Jessie. Soon after the lights were out on Cindy's first night, the girls started fighting. Skeezer, making her rounds, stood in the doorway of the double room until her presence was felt, then she crossed the room and took her stand between the beds. She looked from Cindy to Jessie before she settled down on the floor to spend the night with them. Hands that had been reaching to pull hair, or scratch, reached to pet Skeezer. Goodnights were said, not by the girls to each other, but to Skeezer.

They were all in the day room, some idle, some occupied. Gwen was finishing a picture of Skeezer that she had started drawing earlier in the day. Oriole was standing near the TV, dancing in time with the music. Cindy and Tillie were playing a card game.

Willie-John looked around the room. "Where's Walter?"

"He's gone," Gwen said. "Some people came for him, he's going to be their boy now. They have a farm. Walter is going to help them take care of the animals. Don't you remember when they came last week, and how nice they were?"

Willie-John nodded. "He's lucky, but not so lucky as me. I've got Gretchen."

Skeezer jumped down from the couch and pushed herself against Willie-John, then she sat on her haunches facing Gwen.

"Thanks, Skeezer, now I can see how your brown bib goes under your chin," Gwen's pencil moved with more certainty, "and how long your black whiskers are, and your tan eyebrows."

"Be sure you get her nose right and the way it itches."

"I'll try."

Willie-John watched the artist at work. "Why do you make a picture of Skeezer when you can see her?"

"Because I'm going home for good next week and I want to have a picture of Skeezer for always."

"I'm going soon, too."

"That's nice."

Willie-John looked serious. "Maybe." One part of him longed for home; another part of him that had felt safe at CPH wondered. "I'll miss Skeezer."

"You'll have Gretchen."

"That's right." He squared his shoulders. "It makes a kid happy to have a dog." Leaving Gwen, he moved over to stand beside the table where a card game was going on.

Skeezer followed him, but after a moment decided she had no interest in the game. With a swipe of a paw, she tumbled the cards into a heap on the floor.

"See!" Willie-John exclaimed, "Skeezer can always make you do what she wants to do, and she wants a game."

It was true. Skeezer had been quiet long enough and she did want a game. Cindy and Tillie forgot about the cards and followed Willie-John and Skeezer out to the hall. Aaron soon joined them. Racing up and down, they chased each other and were chased, shouted and laughed. When the fast fun got too much, Skeezer stopped suddenly and threw herself against the nearest person who happened to be Aaron. She turned and walked toward her doghouse, had a long drink of water from the bowl that stood near, then flattened herself against the wall. The participant would now become the observer of whatever else might happen.

Staff blew a whistle, then called that it was time to get ready for supper. "Some of you boys better change your shirts."

Before another month had passed, Willie-John's parents came for him. Standing proudly, with head high and shoulders erect between his father and mother, he could hardly contain his excitement. They had told him that Gretchen was in the car, waiting for him.

At the door Willie-John turned to Skeezer, momentarily overcome by an old loyalty. "I'd like you to meet Gretchen, Skeezer, but if you did you might just push her around the way you do other dogs." He turned to Miss Williams. "Skeezer's happy here, isn't she?"

"Yes, she knows this is where she belongs."

So the big door at the end of the hall opened and closed and Willie-John went out into the world.

In his room on his bed, where Skeezer had often stretched herself out comfortably, was an old shrunken tee shirt with Willie-John's name on it. A piece of paper had been pinned to it, THIS IS FOR SKEEZER.

Gwen had already gone, little changed outwardly but inwardly a new person.

Oriole would go any time, as soon as the right foster home could be found for her. Her parents had willingly agreed to the separation, realizing that they were not capable of giving her the home she should have.

"Going for good," Bentley had said jauntily when his father, now married again, had come for him.

"I'm here for a long time," Rosey Ann commented, cheerfully stating a fact.

"But your parents do take you home every weekend," Miss Williams reminded.

Rosey Ann hopped up and down, smiling elfinly. She knew how lucky she was. "If I weren't here, what would Skeezer do? I know, when I go I'll give her my pink and yellow bunny."

New children came, Benjie and Ellen and Theodore. Skeezer studied them on arrival and at night spent extra time in their rooms, getting used to three new smells and sorting them out in her own way. And there was Martha.

Martha had arrived in a wheelchair, pushed by her father, comforted by her mother; but her parents were the ones who needed comforting. Martha, unable to walk was unable to talk; and she had not eaten normally for a long time. When the pediatric unit had done all possible for her, she was transferred to CPH. Seeing the other children, she put her hands up to her face, covering it, bending her head down.

Compassion, warmed by confidence, was in Miss Williams' voice and manner as she talked with Martha's parents. But the little hands still covered the face even when Martha's mother bent

151

down to kiss her a tearful good-by. Her father laid his hands on her head for a moment. "We love you, honey," he whispered.

That very day in the mail, Skeezer had received a present of an oversized balloon, a beach ball gay with multi-colored stripes and made of something tougher than rubber. It was hung on the wall in Martha's room, high enough so Skeezer would have to jump for it. She did, but couldn't quite get it. However, everytime she jumped, a crack appeared between the fingers covering Martha's face. The head that had been bent almost into her lap lifted slightly, then a little more and a little more, so the eyes could see what was going on.

After a dozen tries, Skeezer got the ball and brought it down, but it was too tough to puncture. She lay beside it panting, proud of her achievement, and proud that her newest charge had witnessed it. Miss Williams placed a cup filled with dry dog food in Martha's hands and left the room. When she returned, the cup was empty and it was obvious who had received its contents. There were crumbs on the floor.

That night Martha ate her supper. Not much, but it was a beginning.

The next day, during a hike along the river, Benjie kept drawing away from the other children to bring up the rear at a dawdling pace. Skeezer bumped and nudged him so often that he finally decided to travel at the pace of the group. No one said anything, no one took any particular notice of Skeezer. She was simply doing what the Shepherd strain in her compelled her to do. Accountable for a flock, she felt bound to fold in with the others the one who lagged or strayed.

When they stopped at one of the drinking fountains for water, Skeezer sat down and watched them.

Ellen said, "The dog wants a drink, too."

Rosey Ann explained, "She'll have one when we get back to CPH."

As soon as they went through the gate into the playground, Skeezer dashed ahead to the drinking fountain at the side of the building. Jumping up against it with her front paws, she waited for someone to turn the knob so she could drink. When it was turned and the water bubbled out, she lapped it.

"See," Oriole said, proud of their dog, "this is the only fountain she's allowed to drink from. It's one of her rules."

Ellen stared. This was something new to her. There had been no rules of any kind in the life she had come from.

Benjie wandered off to sit in the sandbox while two staff lined up teams for a game of baseball. Skeezer walked deliberately toward the sandbox. Near it she stopped and sat down. Benjie was all right where he was. He just wanted to be by himself. Where she was she could keep an eye on him and an eye on the game. In baseball, all wild balls were considered to be Skeezer's and she went after them. She had her own ways and sometimes returned the ball, but if she was bored and wanted a little excitement she made off with it. For the children to get it again meant a chase around the playground until some one of them caught up with her.

Skeezer had shown how she could drink from a fountain. Aaron was determined to show off another accomplishment. When a halt was called in their play for milk and cookies, Aaron drank his and took the empty carton away a short distance and dropped it on the grass.

"Now watch," he commanded, "everybody watch." He called to Skeezer.

She turned to face him, ears cocked, head

slightly tilted. His voice had the tone that meant attention.

"Skeezer," Aaron pointed to the carton, "go pick up that litter and put it in the trash can."

Skeezer looked at him as if to say, "Why me? You put it there."

Aaron repeated his command.

Skeezer walked away from the group. Empty milk cartons were no concern of hers.

Aaron stamped in anger, then he lunged out at the boy nearest him who happened to be Theodore.

"Take it easy kids," a staff stepped between them before a fight could get going. The voice was quiet, the hands firm. "Now, Aaron, go and pick up your own milk carton and put it in the trash where it belongs."

Aaron went off slowly toward the carton, muttering to himself.

"Theodore, tie your shoe laces. "We're going in now."

Rosey Ann had been at the sandbox. With Benjie's help she had filled a little pail with sand.

"I'm going to give this to Martha," she announced as she joined the children on their way into the building, "so's she can play with it until she can come out and play with us."

"Maybe we'll all play with it," Tillie said.

"*With* Martha," Oriole made it clear. Of all that she had learned at CPH, something that she would take with her when she left was the warm memory of the fun they had when they all played together.

Miss Williams, as she often did, was standing at the door to the ward when the children returned.

Rosey Ann told her what the little pail of sand was for.

"That's fine, girls, just fine," she said. "Martha's in her room, but she's waiting to see you."

When evening came and the ward was quiet, Skeezer returned from her rounds to sit by Miss Williams at her desk.

"Someday, Skeezer, we'll be training another dog to take your place."

Skeezer pushed her nose against her friend, then gazed up at her. Sound had drawn her attention; tone promised intimacy.

"It won't be for a long time, Skeezer. You've still got a job to do and you're doing it well, but we have to think of these things."

Skeezer's ears moved back, then forward. It

was her way of saying, "I'm listening."

Miss Williams dropped her hand to rest it on the smooth dark head. "You've taught acceptance to so many, Skeezer, that's because you know something about it yourself: the acceptance that helps us get on with the business of living."

The Author

ELIZABETH YATES is a skilled author who makes her home in the New Hampshire hills near Peterborough. The old farmhouse which she and her husband, William McGreal, had such joy in restoring has seen much living. Its welcome is warm, and made lively by the two Shelties who romp through it, Sir Gibbie and his young playmate Nicky. Her books for both children and adults have received many honors. Notable among them is the Newbery Medal, given in 1951 to *Amos Fortune, Free Man* by the American Library Association as "the most distinguished contribution to American literature for children." Recently, Elizabeth Yates was awarded the Sarah Josepha Hale Medal which is presented annually "to a distinguished author whose work and life reflect the literary tradition of New England."

The Artist

Using her own children and their friends as models for the children portrayed in Skeezer's story, JOAN DRESCHER has captured in her drawings the mood and sensitivity of the narrative. Mrs. Drescher studied art at the Rochester Institute of Technology, Parsons School of Design, and the Art Students League.